Rick Santorum
vs.
Newt Gingrich
On The Issues

Jesse Gordon,
OnTheIssues.org

Table of Contents

Introduction 3

Santorum vs. Gingrich on Domestic Issues........... 7

Mandatory Sentencing...10
Death Penalty 12
Gun Rights 14
Drugs in Society 16
Environmental Protection Agency..18
Environmental Risks..20
Nuclear Waste...22
Environment vs. Economy..24
WikiLeaks 26
Electromagnetic Pulse..28
Transportation Policy...30
Television Censorship...32
Health Mandate...34
Medicare 36
ObamaCare..38

Santorum vs. Gingrich on Economic Issues........41

Financial Bailout...44
Mortgage Crisis 46
Size of Government 48
Regulatory Reform...50
Federal Reserve 52
Balanced Budget 54
Campaign Finance Reform...56
Government Spending..58
Unions...60
Offshore Jobs 62
Social Security Privatization 64
Retirement Age..66
Death Tax 68
Tax Simplification 70
Corporation Policy...72

Santorum vs. Gingrich on Social Issues.................75

Birth Control 78

Abortion Funding 80

Abortion Morality..82

Welfare State..84

Welfare in Contract With America 86

Don't-Ask-Don't-Tell...88

Defense of Marriage Act...90

Churches and Same-Sex Marriage.........................92

Affirmative Action 94

Homeschooling...96

School Vouchers..98

Religion in Schools 100

Church-State Separation 102

American Faith 104

Tea Party...106

Conservative Values 108

Santorum vs. Gingrich on International Issues ..111

Global Warming 114

Oil Drilling...116

China Trade 118

Border Security..120

Guest Workers 122

Pakistani Nukes...124

Israel/Palestine 126

Iranian Sanctions 128

Foreign Aid 130

Patriot Act 132

Defense spending..134

Sources of Terrorism 136

Unconventional Weapons 138

Iraq War..140

Afghanistan War 142

Book reviews 143

A Nation Like No Other, by Speaker Newt Gingrich 146

It Takes a Family, by Rick Santorum 148

A Senator Speaks Out, edited by Monument Press 149

Real Change, by Newt Gingrich 152

Rediscovering God in America, by Newt Gingrich 154

Santorum vs. Gingrich on VoteMatch:...............156

Santorum vs. Gingrich On the Issues

Pundits describe Senator Santorum (R, PA) and Speaker Gingrich (R, GA) as the "conservative alternatives" to Gov. Mitt Romney (R, MA). The post-Iowa caucus Republican presidential primary race also includes Rep. Ron Paul (R, TX) as the libertarian alternative and Gov. Jon Huntsman (R, UT) as the moderate alternative. Santorum and Gingrich uniquely share am underlying political philosophy unlike any other pairing from this group.

This book explores Santorum's and Gingrich's social conservatism and economic conservatism, in the context of being the "conservative alternative" to Gov. Romney, and where it's true or untrue that they are, in fact, the conservative alternative. This book outlines their stances on the issues, in a side-by-side manner for each issue, on many of controversial topics that they will face as President.

We gather the two candidates' issue stances from their political autobiographies; from debates in both the 2011-2012 election season and past elections; from public speeches; from campaign websites; and from political analysis websites. All of the excerpts appear, with many additional issue stances, on our website, www.OnTheIssues.org.

The purpose of this book, and the mission of our website, is to inform voters about candidates' issue stances—what they believe about the issues, and what they have done to implement those beliefs. The mainstream media report on candidates' politics: who's ahead this week; who "won" the last debate; who has endorsed whom. We reject the "horse race politics" that dominates the mainstream media, and instead focus on what matters: Santorum on the issues versus Gingrich on the issues.

—Jesse Gordon, Editor-in-Chief, jesse@OnTheIssues.org
January 2012

Dedication

To Adam, Jamie, & Pete

Acknowledgments

This book would not have been possible without the tireless efforts of the entire OnTheIssues team: Derek Camara, Janice Gordon, Michele Gordon, Peter Hoerr, Ram Lau, Adam Leighton, Jamie Leighton, Naomi Lichtenberg, Ogden Porter, Will Rico, Dan Teittinen, Irma Teittinen, and especially Kathleen Camara.

Santorum vs. Gingrich on Domestic Issues

Domestic issues focus on joint state-federal jurisdiction or enforcement, including the following topics:

- *Crime:* including mandatory sentencing and the death penalty. Sen. Santorum supports criminal rehabilitation, especially by Christian counseling; Rep. Gingrich does not; and both support the death penalty.

- *Gun Control:* Both candidates agree on an individual right rather than a collective right to gun ownership.

- *Drugs:* including marijuana legalization and the War on Drugs. This issue differentiates Santorum's family-based approach versus Gingrich's approach of increased enforcement.

- *Environment:* including pollution and EPA issues. Gingrich demonstrates the classical conservationist attitude; Santorum expresses a pro-nature attitude but votes against the EPA.

- *Technology and Infrastructure:* including high-tech Internet and privacy issues, as well as low-tech roads and bridges investment issues. Gingrich is a futurist on this issue (as he is on many issues). Santorum applies family values to technology, and applies need-based goals for infrastructure.

- *Health Care:* including federal healthcare and ObamaCare issues; plus Medicare/Medicaid and state issues. The two candidates try to outdo each other in opposing ObamaCare (which has become a recurring theme at the GOP primary debates), both offering voluntary and market-based solutions.

Rick Santorum
on Domestic Issues

Santorum on Mandatory Sentencing: 10
    Allow felons to vote again after 5 years crime-free

Santorum on Death Penalty: 12
    YES on limiting death penalty appeals

Santorum on Gun Rights: 14
    YES on prohibiting lawsuits against gun manufacturers

Santorum on Drugs in Society: 16
    Kids living with married parents less likely to use drugs

Santorum on Environmental Protection Agency: 18
    NO on including oil & gas smokestacks in mercury regulations

Santorum on Environmental Risks: 20
    Nature is a subtle web of intricate connections

Santorum on Nuclear Waste: 22
    YES on approving a nuclear waste repository

Santorum on Environment vs. Economy: 24
    Rated 0% by the LCV, indicating anti-environment votes

Santorum on WikiLeaks: 26
    Prosecute WikiLeaks on terrorism charges

Santorum on Electromagnetic Pulse: 28
    Scale of potential destruction from EMP demands action

Santorum on Transportation Policy: 30
    Fund reverse-commuting for distressed suburbs

Santorum on Television Censorship: 32
    Make "airplane" edited movie versions with advisory labels

Santorum on Health Mandate: 34
    If we let states mandate insurance, sterilization is ok too

Santorum on Medicare: 36
    Give Medicare same options and opt-out as Congress

Santorum on ObamaCare: 38
    Liberal states won't waive ObamaCare; we must repeal it

Newt Gingrich
on Domestic Issues

Gingrich on Mandatory Sentencing:..11
    3-strike laws are constitutional; enforce courts compliance

Gingrich on Death Penalty: 13
    Voted NO on replacing death penalty with life imprisonment

Gingrich on Gun Rights: 15
    Don't redefine Constitution with no individual right to arms

Gingrich on Drugs in Society: 17
    Drug-free society focuses on both drug supply & demand

Gingrich on Environmental Protection Agency:.............................19
    Replace EPA with new Environmental Solutions Agency

Gingrich on Environmental Risks:..21
    Greatest enviro dangers are poverty & command bureaucracy

Gingrich on Nuclear Waste:..23
    Put nuclear waste in deep storage for 10,000 years

Gingrich on Environment vs. Economy:..25
    Combine healthy environment and a healthy economy

Gingrich on WikiLeaks:...27
    Treat WikiLeaks as enemy combatants engaged in terrorism

Gingrich on Electromagnetic Pulse:..29
    Prepare more for electromagnetic pulse attack

Gingrich on Transportation Policy: 31
    Establish three high-speed rail corridors; NY-MA; FL; & CA

Gingrich on Television Censorship: 33
    Television is the wasteland of cynicism

Gingrich on Health Mandate: 35
    If you mandate healthcare, you mandate everything in life

Gingrich on Medicare: 37
    Block grant Medicaid; create individual incentives & bonuses

Gingrich on ObamaCare:..39
    Repeal ObamaCare; sign tort reform instead

Santorum on Mandatory Sentencing

Allow felons to vote again after 5 years crime-free

African-American communities are hard hit by crime: the large percentages of black men who become involved in the criminal justice system: 16.2% of blacks will go to prison at some point in their lives, compared to 2.5% of whites. For black males, the number is 28.5%. The impact of these figures upon the community is staggering. Just think what these percentages mean to marriage, to families, and to children. Plus, in many states, convicted felons can never vote, practically ensuring that large numbers of black men are permanently disengaged from civic life. That is why I have supported state laws and even voted for federal laws allowing felons to vote again, provided they have been crime-free for five years.

Source: It Takes a Family, by Sen. Rick Santorum, p. 62, April 30, 2006

Support Prison Fellowship InnerChange Initiative

We pray that convicted felons experience rehabilitation and, if they do, we should grant them forgiveness. Forgiveness is *powerful*— but right now we're withholding our forgiveness, because we never fully welcome the ex-felon back into society.

In four states—TX, IA, KS, & MN—Prison Fellowship runs the InnerChange Freedom Initiative. It's a 24-hour-a-day program that runs for the last 12 to 18 months of a prisoner's sentence, and then at least another 6 months after the prisoner is released.

Source: It Takes a Family, by Sen. Rick Santorum, p. 62, April 30, 2006

Gingrich on Mandatory Sentencing

3-strike laws are constitutional; enforce courts compliance

Anyone who thinks the various decisions of the Supreme Court are not adequately worrisome need only look at the Ninth Circuit Court of Appeals to see how far the Left-liberals will go and how domination by secular Left-liberal judges will change America.

For example, consider the following Ninth Court decisions:

- *Andrade v. Attorney General of California*, (2001): The Ninth Circuit said the California three-strikes law was unconstitutional; the Supreme Court reversed it.

- *Summerlin v. Stewart*, (2003): The Ninth Circuit ruled that death sentences must be enacted by a jury, and not a judge, and that the ruling applied retroactively, voiding the death sentences of over 100 inmates. The Supreme Court reversed the retroactive ruling.

When a court is reversed this often, it clearly fails to meet the "good behavior" test of the Constitution. The good behavior test should be enforced. It would certainly focus the Ninth Circuit's attention on survival rather than radicalism.

Source: Winning the Future, by Newt Gingrich, pp. 58-60, Oct. 1, 2005

NOTE: "Three Strikes" laws mandate that criminal offenders are sentenced to life imprisonment upon their third criminal conviction. The term refers to the baseball rule, "Three Strikes and You're Out."

Santorum on Death Penalty

Voted YES on limiting death penalty appeals

Vote to table, or kill, a motion to send the bill back to the joint House-Senate conference committee with instructions to delete the provisions in the bill that would make it harder for prisoners given the death penalty in state courts to appeal.

Source: Bill S.735 ; vote number 66 on April 17, 1996

Voted NO on replacing death penalty with life imprisonment

Amendment to replace death penalty crimes in the 1994 Omnibus Crime Bill with life imprisonment.

Source: Bill HR 4092 ; vote number 107 on April 14, 1994

NOTE: The death penalty is currently implemented in 34 states. It was re-legalized by a Supreme Court decision in 1977. Since then, 1,278 people have been executed. About 3,250 inmates remain on 'Death Row.' Texas is by far the national leader in executions—it has executed 477 people as of Jan. 2012, 37% of the national total. (Virginia is a very distant second with 109).

Gingrich on Death Penalty

Voted NO on replacing death penalty with life imprisonment

Amendment to replace death penalty crimes in the 1994 Omnibus Crime Bill with life imprisonment.

Source: Bill HR 4092; vote number 107 on April 14, 1994

More prisons, more enforcement, effective death penalty

Gingrich wrote the Contract with America:

[As part of the Contract with America, within 100 days we pledge to bring to the House Floor the following bill]:

The Taking Back Our Streets Act:

An anti-crime package including stronger truth in sentencing, "good faith" exclusionary rule exemptions, effective death penalty provisions, and cuts in social spending from this summer's crime bill to fund prison construction and additional law enforcement to keep people secure in their neighborhoods and kids safe in their schools.

Source: Contract with America on Sept. 27, 1994

Santorum on Gun Rights

Voted YES on prohibiting lawsuits against gun manufacturers

A bill to prohibit civil liability actions from being brought or continued against manufacturers, distributors, dealers, or importers of firearms or ammunition for damages, injunctive or other relief resulting from the misuse of their products by others. Voting YES would:

- Exempt lawsuits brought against individuals who knowingly transfer a firearm that will be used to commit a violent or drug-trafficking crime

- Exempt lawsuits against actions that result in death, physical injury or property damage due solely to a product defect

- Call for the dismissal of all qualified civil liability actions pending on the date of enactment by the court in which the action was brought

- Prohibit the manufacture, import, sale or delivery of armor piercing ammunition, and sets a minimum prison term of 15 years for violations

- Require all licensed importers, manufacturers and dealers who engage in the transfer of handguns to provide secure gun storage or safety devices

Source: Protection of Lawful Commerce in Arms Act; Bill S 397 ;
vote number 219 on July 29, 2005

Gingrich on Gun Rights

Don't redefine Constitution
with no individual right to arms

Over the last 50 years the Supreme Court has become a permanent constitutional convention in which the whims of five appointed lawyers have rewritten the meaning of the Constitution. Under this new, all-powerful model of the Court—and by extension the trail-breaking 9th Circuit Court—the Constitution and the law can be redefined, unchecked, by federal judges.

Anyone who thinks various Supreme Court decisions are not adequately worrisome need only look at the 9th Circuit Court of Appeals to see how domination by secular Left-liberal judges will change America. It is hard to imagine that one court could be so out of step with the views of the vast majority of the American people. And it is unforgivable that this destructive pattern could have been going on for a generation without an effective challenge.

For example, consider the following 9th Court decision: Silveira v. Lockyear, (2002): The 9th Circuit held there is no individual right to keep and bear arms.

Source: Winning the Future, by Newt Gingrich, pp. 57-9, Oct. 1, 2005

NOTES: The "9th Circuit Court" refers to a federal court which is inferior to the Supreme Court. The Supreme Court later ruled on the issue of "individual rights," in the 2008 case called "District of Columbia v. Heller," that the 2nd Amendment does define an individual right to gun ownership, as opposed to a "collective right" for a state-run and state-armed National Guard.

Santorum on Drugs in Society

Kids living with married parents less likely to use drugs

Families set standards and demand that their children live up to them. Strong families are grounded in a code of conduct, morality, values, plus judicious use of the age-old sanctions of shame and stigma. And that last part, by the way—parental *enforcement* of standards. After all, they say, children did not *consent* to their parents' values.

Children living with their married mother and father, as compared to other children, are less likely to get into trouble or use alcohol and drugs. They do better in school; they get better jobs. Teenagers on single-parent households or households with a stepparent are at 1.5 to 2.5 times the risk of using illegal drugs as are teens living with their mother and father.

Source: It Takes a Family, by Sen. Rick Santorum, pp. 18-19&24,
Apr 30, 2006

Bigger drug problem since welfare state started

How many people believe that, in the last 30 years, as a result of the welfare state, the neighborhoods in which people on welfare reside are safer, that crime is less, that the values of the people who are on welfare in second and third generations are better than they were before? Drugs. Are there less drugs? Are drugs less of a problem in these communities than they were 30 years ago? Is the family structure better than it was 30 years ago? The problem is, we are stuck with that system right now. We must—we must—face that and change that.

Source: Santorum speech in "A Senator Speaks Out," p. 42, July 18, 1996

Gingrich on Drugs in Society

Drug-free society focuses on both drug supply & demand

It is essential that we find the means to create a drug-free society for our children. As everyone knows, this has not been an easy matter for us.

The Partnership for a Drug-Free America, with its constant efforts at persuasion & education, and Nancy Reagan's "Just Say No" campaign had a real effect on drug use between 1984 and 1992. In fact, drug use declined by 2/3 in 8 years. Drug use began to rise again when the educational ad campaigns were dumped by the Clinton Administration. Now we have to launch a full-scale torrent of antidrug education, in schools, in churches, in youth organizations, in after-school programs, and everywhere else that young people hang out.

We must also raise the cost of buying and using drugs. We must find a number of economic and social penalties—not just the threat of prison which we know does not work—that will make drug use socially unacceptable. We must seal off the American border by combining [various agencies] into one focused border agency.

Source: Lessons Learned the Hard Way, by Newt Gingrich, pp.204–205, Jul 2, 1998

Santorum on Environmental Protection Agency

Voted NO on including oil & gas smokestacks in mercury regulations

A joint resolution disapproving the rule submitted by the Environmental Protection Agency (EPA) on March 15, 2005, relating to the removal of coal- and oil-fired electric generating units from the list of major sources of hazardous air pollutants under the Clean Air Act. The EPA's Clean Air Mercury RuleLimits smokestack emissions in a two-phase program founded on a market based capping system

Calls for the first cap to limit mercury emissions to 38 tons in 2010

Requires the second and final cap to begin in 2018 and stay fix at 15 tons

Source: EPA's Clean Air Mercury Rule; Bill S J Res 20 ;
vote number 225 on Sept. 13, 2005

Gingrich on Environmental Protection Agency

Replace EPA with new Environmental Solutions Agency

I don't think the EPA bureaucrats, who are dedicated to a Washington centered, top down, bureaucratic control by litigation and regulation, are going learn a new approach, and a new model.

Now a new Environmental Solutions Agency, I believe, would do a better job of both protecting the environment and the economy. I believe that incentives, innovators, and entrepreneurs will solve environmental problems.

The new Environmental Solutions Agency should see communities, states, and industries as partners, not adversaries in solving problems when one approaches. The Environmental Solutions Agency should look for new science, new technologies, and new approaches to get more energy, more jobs, and a better environment simultaneously.

Source: Speech at Conservative Political Action Conference, Feb. 11, 2011

EPA should not regulate dust storms in Iowa

If you look at the EPA's record, it is increasingly radical, it's increasingly imperious, it doesn't cooperate, it doesn't collaborate, and it doesn't take into account economics. In Iowa they had a dust regulation under way because they control particulate matter. They were worried that the plowing of a cornfield would lead dust to go to another farmer's cornfield, and they were planning to issue a regulation. Now, this is an agency out of touch with reality, and you need a new agency that is practical, uses economic factors, and actually incentivizes change, doesn't just punish it.

Source: Meet the Press GOP New Hampshire debate, Jan. 8, 2012

Santorum on Environmental Risks

Nature is a subtle web of intricate connections

Environmental Impact Statements are a sight to behold: realms of scientific data and analysis documenting, or speculating, about environmental effect of a dam or highway through a wetland. While they are costly, and easily abused, they do reflect a true insight: namely, that nature is a subtle web of intricate organic connections, and even small changes in an ecosystem can have large and unintended negative effects downstream. Some call it the "butterfly effect": the mere flapping of a butterfly's wings may contribute to causing a hurricane. Trying to look ahead to what might be lost is simply prudent.

The requirement of Environmental Impact Statements is a result of congressional action after much deliberation. Congress made sure that the public would have input into the process—some say far too much public input. You may or may not like the idea of Environmental Impact Statements, but the idea went through the democratic process and was refined to become what it is today.

Source: It Takes a Family, by Sen. Rick Santorum, pp.217-20,
Apr 30, 2006

Gingrich on Environmental Risks

Greatest environmental dangers are poverty & command bureaucracy

The greatest dangers to biodiversity on the planet today are poor people cutting down tropical forests for money and killing endangered species for meat. Wealthy people can afford to protect the forests and protect endangered species. The greatest areas of pollution and toxic wastes on the planet today are the byproducts of the Soviet Empire and a centralized command bureaucracy that was willing to kill the environment to reach production quotas.

Source: Gingrich Communications website, www.newt.org, "Issues,"
Sep 1, 2007

Reject apocalyptic warnings; they only lead to higher taxes

In addition to favoring science and innovation over red tape and litigation, we must reject an approach to the environment that relies on apocalyptic warnings. In every instance the danger was apocalyptic, science and technology were major threats, and the free market was hazardous. Big government, big regulation, centralized bureaucratic controls, and higher taxes were the solution.

The danger hers is that private property rights & individual liberty could be taken away in favor of some collectivist & non-democratic elite's interpretation of what is needed. The level of power that this would give to international bureaucrats is almost beyond belief.

Source: Real Change, by Newt Gingrich, pp.197–8, Dec. 18, 2007

Santorum on Nuclear Waste

Voted YES on approving a nuclear waste repository

Approval of the interim nuclear waste repository.

The repository would be located at Yucca Mountain in Nevada, with an integrated management system for storage and permanent disposal of spent nuclear fuel and high-level radioactive waste.

Voting YES would authorize the President with sole and unreviewable discretion to determine the suitability of the Yucca Mountain site.

Status: Bill Passed 65-34.

Source: Nuclear Waste Policy Act of 1997; Bill S. 104 ;
vote number 42 on April 15, 1997

NOTE: Yucca Mountain is a federally-owned mountain in Nevada which the federal government has proposed as a long-term repository for nuclear waste. Yucca Mountain was selected because, in theory, it is geologically stable enough to survive intact for the tens of thousands of years until the nuclear waste becomes harmless. The site was first proposed under President Reagan in 1985-1987; Congress approved it under President Bush in 2002; and then Congress canceled the program under President Obama in April 2011.

Gingrich on Nuclear Waste

Put nuclear waste in deep storage for 10,000 years

Q: Do you support opening the national nuclear repository at Yucca Mountain?

GINGRICH: I think that it has to be looked at scientifically. We have to find a safe method of taking care of nuclear waste. Today, because it's been caught up in a political fight, we have small units of nuclear waste all over this country in a way that is vastly more dangerous than finding a method of keeping it in a very, very deep place that would be able to sustain 10,000 or 20,000 or 30,000 years of geological safety.

Q: Is Yucca Mountain that place?

GINGRICH: I'm not a scientist. I mean, Yucca Mountain certainly was picked by the scientific community as one of the safest places in the US.

Q: You were for opening it in Congress, right?

GINGRICH: When I was in Congress, I worked with the Nevada delegation to make sure that there was time for scientific studies. But we have to find some method of finding a very geologically stable place, and most geologists believe that, in fact, Yucca Mountain is that.

Source: GOP primary debate in Las Vegas, Oct. 18, 2011

Santorum on Environment vs. Economy

Scores 0% by the LCV on environmental issues

The League of Conservation Voters (LCV) is the political voice of the national environmental movement and the only organization devoted full-time to shaping a pro-environment Congress and White House. We run tough and effective campaigns to defeat anti-environment candidates, and support those leaders who stand up for a clean, healthy future for America.

Through our National Environmental Scorecard and Presidential Report Card we hold Congress and the Administration accountable for their actions on the environment. Through regional offices, we build coalitions, promote grassroots power, and train the next generation of environmental leaders. The 2003 National Environmental Scorecard provides objective, factual information about the environmental voting records of all Members of the first session of the 108th Congress.

This Scorecard represents the consensus of experts from 20 respected environmental and conservation organizations who selected the key votes on which Members of Congress should be graded. LCV scores votes on the most important issues of the year, including environmental health and safety protections, resource conservation, and spending for environmental programs. Scores are calculated by dividing the number of pro-environment votes by the total number of votes scored.

The votes included in this Scorecard presented Members of Congress with a real choice on protecting the environment and help distinguish which legislators are working for environmental protection.

Source: LCV website on Dec. 31, 2003

Gingrich on Environment vs. Economy

Combine healthy environment and a healthy economy

It is possible to have a healthy environment & a healthy economy. It is possible to build incentives for a cleaner future. It is possible to have biodiversity & wealthy human beings on the same planet. And it is possible to have free markets, scientific and technological advances, and an even more positive environmental outcome. There is every reason to be optimistic that if we develop smart environmental and biodiversity policies our children & grandchildren will experience an even more pleasant world.

Source: Gingrich Communications website, www.newt.org, Dec. 1, 2006

Santorum on WikiLeaks

Prosecute WikiLeaks on terrorism charges

Sarah Palin asked why the White House had not issued orders to tighten security back in July, when WikiLeaks released thousands of classified military documents on Afghanistan. "What explains this strange lack of urgency on their part?"

Palin concluded: "We are at war. American soldiers are in Afghanistan fighting to protect our freedoms. They are serious about keeping America safe. It would be great if they could count on their government being equally serious about that vital task."

Rick Santorum, another prominent conservative, agreed with her, saying: "We haven't gone after this guy, we haven't tried to prosecute him, we haven't gotten our allies to go out and lock this guy up and bring him up on terrorism charges."

The Obama administration has said that it "deeply regrets" the leaking of the embarrassing cables that have disclosed exactly what American diplomats think of foreign leaders and promised to take "aggressive steps" against those who "stole" them.

Source: Martin Beckford in The Telegraph (U.K.), "Hunt WikiLeaks,"
Nov. 30, 2010

NOTE: WikiLeaks is a website run by a libertarian technophile Julian Assange. In 2010, WikiLeaks got hold of millions of classified government documents that he and his organization believed should not be kept secret from the public. Many of those documents were posted on the WikiLeaks website. Assange has been under criminal investigation ever since.

Gingrich on WikiLeaks

Treat WikiLeaks as enemy combatants engaged in terrorism

Q: If you were in charge, how would you handle Julian Assange and WikiLeaks?

A: Information warfare is warfare, and Julian Assange is engaged in warfare. Information terrorism, which leads to people getting killed, is terrorism, and Julian Assange is engaged in terrorism. He should be treated as an enemy combatant. WikiLeaks should be closed down permanently and decisively. But even more, how can these documents have been released?

Q: Via a private in the Army.

A: How do you have a system so stupid [that an Army Private can] download a quarter million documents and the system doesn't say [anything]? I mean this is a system so stupid that it ought to be a scandal of the first order. This administration is so shallow, and so amateurish about national security that it is painful and dangerous.

Source: Fox News interview on Business Insider, Dec. 5, 2010

Santorum on Electromagnetic Pulse

Scale of potential destruction from EMP demands action

An electromagnetic pulse, or EMP, could be triggered by one or more nuclear warheads exploded more than 100 miles above the United States. Imagine a continent-sized, invisible lightning strike, only more devastating. To those not in a car or plane, it would resemble a power outage at first; nothing electrical would work.

But according to the Electromagnetic Pulse Commission, it would fry our electrical grid, as well as most devices with electronic components, including motor vehicles and backup generators. It could be months, maybe even years, before power is restored and vehicles are repaired.

So is the government taking the threat seriously? Well, the government has taken steps to "harden" senior leadership communications in Washington against an EMP attack. But the Department of Homeland Security doesn't include it on its list of potential threats. The probability and fallout of such an attack are debatable, but the scale of potential destruction demands action now.

Here is something the big spenders from one end of Pennsylvania Avenue to the other will be glad to hear: We need to spend money to study the electromagnetic pulse threat; to help states, localities, and families prepare; and to protect our critical electric infrastructure and transportation networks now.

America's enemies know our Achilles' heel and are no doubt planning to exploit it. The government is wise to protect our senior leadership. Now how about the rest of us?

Source: Article by Santorum in Philadelphia Inquirer, Aug. 27, 2009

Gingrich on Electromagnetic Pulse

Prepare more for electromagnetic pulse attack

Q: What national security issue do you worry about that nobody is asking about?

CAIN: Having been a ballistics analyst and a computer scientist early in my career, cyber-attacks: that's something that we do not talk enough about, and I happen to believe that that is a national security area that we do need to be concerned about.

GINGRICH: I helped create the Hart-Rudman Commission with President Clinton, and they came back after three years and said the greatest threat to the United States was the weapon of mass destruction in an American city, probably from a terrorist. That was before 9/11. That's one of the three great threats. The second is an electromagnetic pulse attack which would literally destroy the country's capacity to function. And the third, as Herman just said, is a cyber attack. All three of those are outside the current capacity of our system to deal with.

Source: CNN National Security GOP primary debate, Nov. 22, 2011

NOTE: An EMP (electromagnetic pulse) is caused by a nuclear weapon detonated at high altitude, which would shut down electrical power and electronic devices over a large area.

Santorum on Transportation Policy

Fund reverse-commuting for distressed suburbs

The Reverse Commuting Program that I authored in 1996 along with Sen. Carol Mosley Braun (D, IL) ensures that people who live in reclamation and distressed areas have opportunity to get where economic opportunity currently resides.

Too many mass-transit commuter routes are designed only to bring people from a metropolitan area into the urban business district. But in many cases, jobs for low-skill workers have migrated to the suburban ring around the city. Unlike suburbanites, most of the urban poor do not have cars. Without some means of transportation, these jobs are literally out of reach.

Federal reverse-commuting dollars help subsidize routes from reclamation areas to suburban job centers. And slowly, the economic benefits of that neighborhood may begin to seep into that reclamation area next door; if not, then economic incentives will result in residents leaving the reclamation area. Then, building on the base of the transitioning-up neighborhood, you begin to gut and rebuild the worse-off area.

Source: It Takes a Family, by Sen. Rick Santorum, p.179, April 30, 2006

Gingrich on Transportation Policy

Establish three high-speed rail corridors;
NY-MA; FL; & CA

The French & Japanese have made substantial investments in creating high-speed rail corridors. The Chinese are now following their lead. The US has 3 corridors that are very conducive to this kind of high-speed train investment. We could build a system between Boston and Washington; from Miami to Tampa, Orlando and Jacksonville; and from San Diego to San Francisco.

There are three problems with trying to build high-speed systems in the US and, not surprisingly, all three relate to government.

1. Union work rules make it impossible, at least if Amtrak has anything to do with it.

2. Pork barrel politicians waste money subsidizing absurdly uneconomic routes

3. Regulations and litigation involved in large-scale construction have become time- consuming and expensive.

I support a 21st century rail system that is privately built, run efficiently, and capable of earning its own way. The US should have a railroad system that works for us, and not for the Amtrak bureaucracy and their unions.

Source: Real Change, by Newt Gingrich, pp.211-2, Dec. 18, 2007

Santorum on Television Censorship

Make "airplane" edited movie versions with advisory labels

The Recording Industry Association of America, prodded by the FTC, now stickers music CDs with "parental advisory" labels if they contain content inappropriate for children. I view such stickers as a red light for my kids. The answer is simple if they were to ask about a CD with that sticker: "No."

There are a number of technical tools available to parents. The industry, however, has responded to these new technological aids with lawsuits and other threats. Rather than trying to take away tools from parents who want to let their kids watch movies (would they rather we just say "No" completely?), the industry should be working with parents to make available to us the "airplane" edited version of their films. A recent poll found that almost three out of four respondents would purchase or rent an airplane-edited version of certain films that they would otherwise choose not to watch at all. Making these films available would be in the economic interest of the industry.

Source: It Takes a Family, by Sen. Rick Santorum, p.327–328,
Apr 30, 2006

Gingrich on Television Censorship

Television is the wasteland of cynicism

Gingrich is fond of putting himself in the place of the inner-city seven-year-old, a child used to violence, in a home without books, and, in too many cases, an unhappy young mother. The child watches television programs that portray businessmen as evil, politicians on the take, and policemen taking bribes. (He calls television "the wasteland of cynicism.") "If you're a little kid today who reads too much or speaks English that's too good, you get beaten up."

Source: Newt!, by Dick Williams, p. 53, June 1, 1995

Santorum on Health Mandate

If we let states mandate insurance, sterilization is ok too

Q: [to Ron Paul]: Does a state has a constitutional right to make someone buy insurance just because they're a resident [as RomneyCare does]?

PAUL: The federal government can't go in and prohibit the states from doing bad things. And I would consider that a very bad thing, but they do have that leeway under our Constitution.

SANTORUM: This is the 10th Amendment run amok. We have Ron Paul saying, oh, whatever the states want to do under the 10th Amendment's fine. So if the states want to pass polygamy, that's fine. If the states want to impose sterilization, that's fine. No, our country is based on moral laws. There are things the states can't do. Abraham Lincoln said the states do not have the right to do wrong. I respect the 10th Amendment, but we are a nation that has values. We are a nation that was built on a moral enterprise, and states don't have the right to tramp over those because of the 10th Amendment.

Source: Iowa Straw Poll GOP debate in Ames Iowa, Aug. 11, 2011

Gingrich on Health Mandate

If you mandate healthcare, you mandate everything in life

Q: You've been very open to the individual mandate. It has become a litmus test in this Republican primary. Should it be?

A: Yes, it should be. If you explore the mandate, it ultimately ends up with unconstitutional powers. It allows the government to define virtually everything. And if you can do it for health care, you can do it for everything in your life, and, therefore, we should not have a mandate.

But I want to answer at a different level. This campaign cannot be only about the presidency. We need to pick up at least 12 seats in the Senate and 30 or 40 more seats in the House, because if you are serious about repealing Obamacare, you have to be serious about building a big enough majority in the legislative branch that you could actually in the first 90 days pass the legislation. So I just think it's very important to understand, it's not about what one person in America does. It's about what the American people do. And that requires a senatorial majority, as well as a presidency.

Source: GOP primary debate in Manchester NH, June 13, 2011

Santorum on Medicare

Give Medicare same options and opt-out as Congress

Q: Rep. Paul Ryan had a plan where he'd like to move seniors off Medicare, give them a voucher or premium support, and then they would take care of their health care from there. You said seniors should be affected right now, 55 plus, have them affected right now?

SANTORUM: I hear this all the time: "We should have the same kind of health care the members of Congress have." Well, that's pretty much what Paul Ryan's plan is. The members of Congress have a premium support model. So does every other federal employee. The federal government has a whole bunch of different options available. If you want a more expensive plan, you pay more of a co-insurance. If you want a less expensive plan, you don't. But fundamental difference between Barack Obama's: it's whether you believe people can be free to make choices or whether you have to make decisions for them. And I believe seniors, just like every other American, should be free to make the choices in their healthcare plan that's best for them.

Source: Meet the Press GOP New Hampshire debate, Jan. 8, 2012

Gingrich on Medicare

Block grant Medicaid; create individual incentives & bonuses

Q: What about Medicaid?

GINGRICH: Go to Newt.org for the proposed 21st Century Contract with America. The first step is to repeal Obamacare. [Then] block grant Medicaid. And block grant all remaining welfare programs. Give the states the power to deal with the poor using innovation and money savings.

I do not believe you solve problems under the Left's policy of people being helpless. We need to rethink Medicaid much the way we rethought welfare reform. Governor Bush in Florida had a program where people who took care of themselves and didn't go to the emergency room got a Christmas bonus. To the shock of academics, poor people were aware of money and strived to get that bonus by not abusing the emergency rooms.

If you had the ability to triage and send people to minute clinics, then the hospital wouldn't charge emergency room rates. We have to start distinguishing between the taxpayer who is concerned with charitable care and taxpayers who are suckers and are being exploited.

Source: Head-to-head debate between Herman Cain & Newt Gingrich, Nov 5, 2011

Santorum on ObamaCare

Liberal states won't waive ObamaCare; we must repeal it

We need to repeal ObamaCare. That's the first thing we need to do. Repeal ObamaCare—we can do it, not by waivers. That's the wrong idea. California going to waive that? No. NY going to waive it? No. All these states—many of them, liberal states—are going to continue on, and then states like NH that will waive it will end up subsidizing California. We need to repeal it by doing it through a reconciliation process, and since I have the experience and know how to do that, we'll get it rid of it.

Source: GOP debate at Dartmouth College, NH, Oct. 11, 2011

First Executive Order: suspend ObamaCare

Q: What would be your first executive order after the disastrous Obama presidency?

A: To suspend all spending on the implementation of Obamacare. Thank you for this opportunity & for fighting for Life, Liberty & the Pursuit of Happiness. I wish the other candidates were here. Please join the fight to save our country at ricksantorum.com

Source: Republican primary debate on Twitter.com, July 21, 2011

Gingrich on ObamaCare

Repeal ObamaCare; sign tort reform instead

President Obama could be bipartisan. There are seven steps to the center for Obama.

1. Sign the repeal of ObamaCare. 58% of the American people, in the most recent poll, favor repeal of ObamaCare.

2. Sign Tort reform for doctors. He said the other night he would like to do it, let's let him do it.

3. Sign the permanent repeal of the death tax.

4. Sign a new Hyde Amendment, so no tax payer money funds abortion in the United States.

5. Sign a new Conservative Budget Act, to control spending and move to a balanced budget.

6. Sign a law to decisively control the border now.

7. Sign a tenth amendment implementation act returning power from Washington to the states and to the people thereof. And that act should include—to prove how real it is—block-granting Medicaid so that states can control the cost and improve the quality without interference from Washington bureaucrats.

Now, I hope you'd agree with me that a President Obama that did those seven things would have come to the center.

Source: Speech at Conservative Political Action Conference, Feb 11, 2011

Santorum vs. Gingrich on Economic Issues

Economic issues focus on the recession recovery and all fiscal matters, including the following topics:

- *Budget & Economy:* including deficit spending and all aspects of the federal budget. Gingrich focuses on supply-side solutions. Santorum supported Fannie & Freddie while in the Senate but now opposes the mortgage bailout.

- *Corporations:* including corporate taxation and corporate welfare. Santorum focuses on reducing corporate taxes and regulations, while Gingrich focuses on applying business methods to government.

- *Government Reform:* focusing on the size of the federal government, which Santorum and Gingrich agree should be smaller and more restricted. Much of Gingrich's "Contract With America" focused on this topic; Gingrich continues that focus today. Santorum instead focuses outside government.

- *Jobs:* including unemployment and union issues. The two candidates agree on right-to-work and on repatriating offshore jobs via corporate tax incentives.

- *Social Security:* including the current Trust Fund and changes for the future. The two candidates agree on providing opt-out mechanisms, but both avoid calling it "privatization."

- *Tax Reform:* including income taxes, tax rates, and bracket redistribution. The two candidates agree on radically reducing taxes; flattening and simplifying the tax code; and on removing the Death Tax.

Rick Santorum
on Economic Issues

Santorum on Financial Bailout: 44
    TARP was biggest government intrusion into private sector

Santorum on Mortgage Crisis: 46
    2005: Fannie & Freddie should create housing affordability

Santorum on Size of Government: 48
    Gov't has averaged 18% of GDP and we're now at 25%

Santorum on Regulatory Reform: 50
    Overturn & freeze all Obama regulations in process

Santorum on Federal Reserve: 52
    Audit the Fed; but no gold standard

Santorum on Balanced Budget: 54
    DC doesn't work; ratify the Balanced Budget Amendment

Santorum on Campaign Finance Reform: 56
    Campaign finance should be purely voluntary

Santorum on Government Spending: 58
    Spend-o-meter: track spending on all Senate amendments

Santorum on Right-to-Work: 60
    Unions good community members but we need right-to-work

Santorum on Offshore Jobs: 62
    Offshore jobs return if you repeal manufacturing regulations

Santorum on Social Security Privatization: 64
    Supports privatization if voluntary

Santorum on Retirement Age: 66
    Raise retirement age? Maybe. Private investment? Yes

Santorum on Death Tax: 68
    Changing estate tax would cost $100B, not save $730B

Santorum on Tax Simplification: 70
    Simplify tax code: just 5 deductions; everything else goes

Santorum on Corporation Policy: 72
    Cut all corporate tax rates to zero

Newt Gingrich
on Economic Issues

Gingrich on Financial Bailout: 45
    Insure banks rather than pass out checks

Gingrich on Mortgage Crisis: 47
    Don't bail out Freddie Mac & Fannie Mae; break them up

Gingrich on Size of Government: 49
    The era of big government is over, and I mean it

Gingrich on Regulatory Reform: 51
    Abolish all White House Czars

Gingrich on Federal Reserve: 53
    The Fed's secrecy & power are antithetical to a free society

Gingrich on Balanced Budget: 55
    Demand a Balanced Budget amendment

Gingrich on Campaign Finance Reform:..57
    Increase federal limits on individual campaign contributions

Gingrich on Government Spending:..59
    Democrats say they oppose earmarks, but proposed 8,000

Gingrich on Right-to-Work: 61
    Defund National Labor Relations Board; favor right-to-work

Gingrich on Offshore Jobs: 63
    2002 Sarbanes-Oxley Act drives IPOs out of the US

Gingrich on Social Security Privatization: 65
    Take Social Security off federal budget; give young a choice

Gingrich on Retirement Age:..67
    Take away politicians' power & control over our retirement

Gingrich on Death Tax:..69
    Death tax is a direct assault on civil society

Gingrich on Tax Simplification:..71
    Adopt a single-rate tax system

Gingrich on Corporation Policy:..73
    Businesses focus on customers; apply Lean Six Sigma to gov't

Santorum on Financial Bailout

TARP was biggest government intrusion into private sector

I opposed the single biggest government intrusion into the private sector, the Wall Street bailout, the TARP program. I opposed it because it violated the principles of our Constitution, the spirit of our Constitution, because the experience I had, that if you open up the door of government involvement in the private sector, some president will, and in fact did, drive a truck through it and explode the size of the federal government and constrict our freedom.

The four people on this panel that actually supported TARP at the time of its passage are the people who say that they are the anti-Washington candidates, that they are the business candidates, and they're the four on this program that supported the Washington bailout, giving Washington—naively, I would say—tools to constrict our freedom.

The four people were Governor Huntsman, Governor Perry, Herman Cain and Governor Romney: all supported TARP.

Source: GOP debate at Dartmouth College, NH, Oct. 11, 2011

Gingrich on Financial Bailout

Insure banks rather than pass out checks

The Path to Socialist Banking:

1. In Sep. 2008, the major brokerage houses teeter on the brink of bankruptcy.

2. President Bush and his Treasury secretary propose a huge bailout to inject $700 billion of capital into falling financial institutions to stabilize them and stop a run on their assets. The plan is called Troubled Assets Relief Program (TARP).

3. Republicans in the House try to stop the bill (they had the majority then) and substitute an approach masterminded by former House speaker Newt Gingrich to insure banks rather than pass out checks to them. The House defeats the Bush bailout proposal.

4. John McCain "suspends" his campaign; the Republicans in the House cave in at the behest of their nominee and agree to TARP.

5. Democrats ask, what will the taxpayer get out of the TARP bailouts? Had the Republicans listened to Gingrich, the question would have had no force, since no money would have changed hands. But in the context of the Bush TARP bill, the question demands an answer.

Source: Take Back America, by Dick Morris, pp.103-5, April 13, 2010

Santorum on Mortgage Crisis

2005: Fannie & Freddie
should create housing affordability

In his eight years on the Senate Banking Committee, there was one issue where Santorum sought to play a leading role. Santorum, despite his reputation as a conservative stalwart, had a keen interest in providing disadvantaged families greater access to affordable housing.

In 2005, when Banking Committee Republicans were trying to tighten the regulation of Fannie Mae and Freddie Mac, Santorum pushed to include language in the legislation that would strengthen their affordable-housing goals. "We're very concerned about making sure that we do things in working with this legislation to improve the access to affordable housing," Santorum said during a July 2005 hearing. He wanted to orient Fannie and Freddie "toward taking a more active role in creating housing opportunities for low and moderate income families."

But 6 years later, GOP presidential candidates say Fannie & Freddie should have been far less oriented toward providing affordable housing—not more so, as Santorum was advocating.

Source: Kevin Wack in "American Banker,"
"Santorum Runs from Record," Jan. 9, 2012

Gingrich on Mortgage Crisis

Don't bail out Freddie Mac & Fannie Mae; break them up

Rep. PAUL: [to Gingrich]: He received a lot of money from Freddie Mac. While he was earning a lot of money from Freddie Mac, I was fighting over a decade to try to explain to people where the housing bubble was coming from. So Freddie Mac is bailed out by the tax payers. So in a way, Newt, I think you probably got some of our tax payer's money.

GINGRICH: First, the housing bubble came from the Federal Reserve inflating the money supply. Second, I was never a spokesman for any agency, I never did any lobbying for any agency. I offered strategic advice. I was in the private sector. You're allowed to charge money for it. It's called free enterprise. I'm not for bailing them out, in fact, I'm for breaking them up.

Q: Rep. Bachmann, you called Speaker Gingrich a "poster boy of crony capitalism."

BACHMANN: When you're taking over $100 million to influence the outcome of legislation in Washington, that's the epitome of a consummate insider.

Source: Yahoo's "Your Voice Your Vote" debate in Iowa, Dec. 10, 2011

NOTE: "Fannie & Freddie" refer to the Federal National Mortgage Association (FNMA, Fannie Mae) and Federal Home Loan Mortgage Corporation (FHLMC, Freddie Mac). Fannie and Freddie were "GSEs"—government-sponsored enterprises—half-private, half-federal, until 2008, when they were placed under full federal control. Their role is to assist banks with creating individual mortgages.

Santorum on Size of Government

Government has averaged 18% of GDP
and we're now at 25%

Q: The deficit cutting super committee is now getting to work. Democrats will demand that savings come from a combination of spending cuts and tax increases, maybe $3 in cuts for every $1 in higher taxes. Is there any ratio of cuts to taxes that you would accept? Three to one? Or even 10 to one?

A: No. The answer is no, because that's not the problem. The problem is that we have spending that has exploded. Government has averaged 18% of GDP as a percentage of the overall economy that government eats up. And we're now at almost 25%. So if you look at where the problem is, it is in spending, not taxes. And we'll get those taxes up if we grow the economy. I put forward the plan to grow the economy and I've provided leadership in the past to get bipartisan things done.

Q: But just confirming, Senator, you would not negotiate on raising taxes?

A: Absolutely not, because it's not the problem. We need to get the economy growing. That doesn't mean taking more money out of it.

Source: Iowa Straw Poll GOP debate in Ames Iowa, Aug. 11, 2011

Gingrich on Size of Government

The era of big government is over, and I mean it

As conservatives we know replacing a Democrat with a Republican is not enough to return America back to job creation and balanced budgets. If I am elected, the next time a president says the era of big government is over, he'll mean it.

Source: Republican primary debate on Twitter.com, July 21, 2011

Modernizing government would save $500B per year in waste

Q: How do you balance the budget, when so much of the budget goes to defense and entitlements?

GINGRICH: That's just a Washington mythology. Anybody who knows anything about the federal government knows that there's such an enormous volume of waste, that if you simply had a serious all-all effort to modernize the federal government, you would have hundreds of billions of dollars of savings falling off. If you modernize the federal government, you save $500 billion a year. One example, the federal government is such a bad manager of money, that somewhere between $70 billion and $120 billion a year in Medicare and Medicaid is paid to crooks. We wrote a book several years ago called "Stop Paying the Crooks." I thought it was pretty obvious even for Washington. So I would start to balance the budget by stop paying the crooks, not by cheating honest Americans.

Source: GOP Tea Party debate in Tampa FL, Sept. 12, 2011

Santorum on Regulatory Reform

Overturn & freeze all Obama regulations in process

Q: As President, if you could enact any policy to fix the economy without congressional approval what would it be?

A: Refuse to spend the money to implement Obamacare. I would freeze all Obama regulations in process and overturn any antibusiness executive order. I would tell the businesses around the world America is open for business and you have a president who wants you here!

Source: Republican primary debate on Twitter.com, July 21, 2011

Companies run into a stiff headwind called government

Q: What about job creation?

SANTORUM: I come from southwestern Pennsylvania, the heart of the steel country, the heart of manufacturing. And it's been devastated because we are uncompetitive. Thirty years ago we were devastated because business and labor didn't understand global competitiveness and we lost a lot of jobs. That's not what's happening now. But they're running into a stiff headwind called government. And it's government taxation, 35% corporate tax which is high—the highest in the world.

Q: Everyone on this stage is for lowering the corporate tax.

SANTORUM: No one wants to zero it out for manufacturers and processors, which is what I do because we are at 20% cost differential with our nine top trading partners on average.

Source: WMUR GOP New Hampshire debate, Jan. 7, 2012

Gingrich on Regulatory Reform

Abolish all White House Czars

Q: As President, if you could enact any policy to fix the economy without congressional approval what would it be?

A: I wouldn't even if I could because congressional passage offers legitimacy of the consent of the governed to the law. Big impact can be made with executive orders though. I would stop EPA from regulating carbon & abolish all White House Czars.

Source: Republican primary debate on Twitter.com, July 21, 2011

NOTE: The term "czar" refers to a powerful presidential appointee who is not confirmed by the Senate. In other words, a "czar" is answerable only to the President, unlike normal Cabinet secretaries and other appointees, who must pass the Senate confirmation process. "Czar" is an informal title used by the press and sometimes by the appointee. For example, Elizabeth Warren was known as the "Consumer Czar," but her formal title was "Special Advisor for the Consumer Financial Protection Bureau." Czars were popularized by Pres. Clinton and the czar count increased to several dozen under Pres. George W. Bush and Pres. Obama, but the practice goes back to the 1930s.

Santorum on Federal Reserve

Audit the Fed; but no gold standard

Q: You said that you were "the Tea Party before there was a Tea Party." But a top Tea Party goal, particularly in Iowa, is to revert back to the gold standard, something you oppose.

SANTORUM: Well, first off, I didn't say that, the Washington Post said it. I simply commented on what they said. I think most of the Tea Party people think their leadership is among the people, not a member of congress. I think there's some reforms we can do at the Fed. And I agree we need to audit the Fed. I disagree with most of what Ron Paul says. Just because he's mostly wrong, doesn't mean he's always wrong. I appreciate his contribution in that regard.

Source: Iowa Straw Poll 2011 GOP debate in Ames Iowa, Aug. 11, 2011

Focus the Fed on sound money, rather than job creation

Q: What is your position on the Federal Reserve?

A: What we should do with the Fed is to make it a single charter instead of a dual charter. I think the second charter that was instituted that had it be responsible for increasing employment and dealing with that leads to a fundamental distrust among the American people that they are taking their eye off the ball, which is sound money. They should be a sound money Federal Reserve. That should be their single charter, and that is it.

Source: Tea Party debate in Tampa FL, Sept. 12, 2011

Gingrich on Federal Reserve

The Fed's secrecy & power
are antithetical to a free society

Q: The chairman of the Federal Reserve, Ben Bernanke, will come to the end of his term in 2014. Would you reappoint Ben Bernanke?

GINGRICH: I would fire him tomorrow.

Q: Why?

GINGRICH: I think he's been the most inflationary, dangerous, and power-centered chairman of the Fed in the history of the Fed. I think the Fed should be audited. I think the amount of money that he has shifted around in secret, with no responsibility, no accountability, no transparency, is absolutely antithetical to a free society. And I think his policies have deepened the depression, lengthened the problems, increased the cost of gasoline, and been a disaster.

Source: 2011 GOP debate in Simi Valley CA at the Reagan Library,
Sep 7, 2011

Santorum on Balanced Budget

DC doesn't work;
ratify the Balanced Budget Amendment

Q: As president, how will you avoid continually raising the debt ceiling?

GINGRICH: We don't need Obama's "balanced approach" (code for raise taxes). We need a balanced budget.

SANTORUM: Pass the Balanced Budget Amendment and work for its ratification across the country!

GINGRICH: When you balance the budget there is no need to raise the debt ceiling. I am the only candidate who has balanced the budget.

JOHNSON: I'd avoid continually raising the debt ceiling by not incurring more debt! I'd submit to Congress a balanced budget in 2013, & veto any appropriation that exceeds that budget.

SANTORUM: DC doesn't work; we need to impose discipline on politicians who want to buy their reelection with your money. BBA is the only way.

GINGRICH: We can balance the budget again by growing the economy, cutting spending and reforming government. That's how we did it before. We CAN do it again.

Source: Republican primary debate on Twitter.com, July 21, 2011

Gingrich on Balanced Budget

Demand a Balanced Budget Amendment

Gingrich signed the Contract From America

The Contract from America, clause 3:

Demand a Balanced Budget:

Begin the Constitutional amendment process to require a balanced budget with a two-thirds majority needed for any tax hike.

The Contract from America, clause 6:

End Runaway Government Spending:

Impose a statutory cap limiting the annual growth in total federal spending to the sum of the inflation rate plus the percentage of population growth.

Source: The Contract From America, July 8, 2010

Santorum on Campaign Finance Reform

Campaign finance should be purely voluntary

The general philosophy of those of us who oppose the McCain-Feingold approach is that we believe that we can fix the campaign finance system in this country by making it purely voluntary, so that no one is going to be forced to contribute to an election.

That is something that you would think is as fundamental as any right that we have in this country, that you should not be forced by your employer, by your union, by your association, or by your family to contribute to anyone the resources that you have worked hard to earn.

So, one general tenet is that contributing to campaigns must be completely voluntary. I think this is a tenet you would suspect would be universally shared. It is not universally shared. People in support of McCain-Feingold, by and large—there are some exceptions, but few—do not support the concept that campaign contributions should be voluntary.

Source: Santorum speech in "A Senator Speaks Out," p.110, Oct. 1, 1997

NOTE: "McCain-Feingold" refers to the Bipartisan Campaign Reform Act of 2002, also known as BCRA, named after its sponsors, Sen. John McCain (R, AZ) and Sen. Russ Feingold (D, WI). McCain-Feingold doubled the campaign donation limit from $1,000 per person to $2,000 per person ($2,500 in 2012), known as "hard money." The law banned "soft money" contributions to political parties, but later Supreme Court cases, particularly "Citizens United," allowed unlimited soft money for purposes of advertising for or against a candidate as long as there was no "coordination" with the campaign.

Gingrich on Campaign Finance Reform

Increase federal limits on individual campaign contributions

Gingrich indicated the principles he would support regarding campaign finance reform:

- Support legislation that would increase the federal limits on individual contributions.

- Strengthen and enforce legislation that encourages full and timely disclosure of campaign finance information.

- Prohibit non-U.S. citizens from making contributions to federal campaigns.

Source: Congressional National Political Awareness Test,
Nov 1, 1998

Santorum on Government Spending

Spend-o-meter:
track spending on all Senate amendments

PAUL: [to Santorum]: I believe Congress should designate how money should be spent. I always voted against spending. You're a big spender; that's all there is to it. You're a big-government conservative. So to say you're a conservative, I think, is a stretch. But you've convinced a lot of people of it, so somebody has to point out your record.

SANTORUM: I've convinced a lot of people of it because my record is actually pretty darn good. I supported and voted for a balanced budget amendment, the line-item veto. In fact, I used to keep track when I was in the Senate of all the amendments that increased spending. I put them on something called a spend-o-meter. If you look at my spending record and you take all the "spending groups," I was rated at the top or near the top every single year, particularly in defense.

Source: WMUR GOP New Hampshire debate, Jan. 7, 2012

Gingrich on Government Spending

Democrats say they oppose earmarks, but proposed 8,000

I listened carefully to the President's speech the other night. Obama suggests to us that he is opposed to earmarks, when the very next day the Democrats are going to bring up a bill with 8,000 earmarks in it and then to suggest that one doesn't count because they started all the pork before he got here. I was looking for change we can believe in.

And so I was startled that he was saying to us that he opposed to earmarks; [I suppose maybe] later he'll really oppose them.

Source: Speech to 2009 Conservative Political Action Conference,
Feb 27, 2009

NOTE: "Earmarks" refers to itemized spending in legislation, i.e., funding targeted toward a particular project in a particular place. The controversy comes about because often the particular place includes the home district of the legislator writing or sponsoring the bill (which is known derisively as "Pork-Barrel Spending"). Earmarks are currently legal and are generally considered ethical; earmark reform focuses on publicizing their existence and perhaps on a future Line Item Veto to remove some.

Santorum on Right-to-Work

Unions are good community members but we need right-to-work

Q: [to Perry]: Do you support "right to work" laws on the federal level?

PERRY: Actually, it's a federal issue because of the law that was passed that forces the states to make a decision about whether or not they're going to be right to work. I'm a right to work guy.

SANTORUM: I have signed a pledge that I would support a national right to work. When I was a senator from Pennsylvania, I didn't vote for it because Pennsylvania's not a right to work state, and I didn't want to vote for a law that would change the law in Pennsylvania, number one. Number two, what can unions do? They can do training. They also do a lot in the community. I work with a lot of labor unions in Philadelphia and other places to do a lot of community involvement work and they try to participate as good members of the community like the business does.

Source: Meet the Press GOP New Hampshire debate, Jan. 8, 2012

NOTE: "Right-to-Work" refers to a state law against requiring union membership. The opposite is a "union shop," where employees are required to pay union dues as a condition for working. 22 states are "right-to-work" states (mostly in the South and West) and 28 are not. A "national right-to-work law" would abolish union shops, and convert them all to "open shops," where employees may join the union voluntarily but are not required.

Gingrich on Right-to-Work

Defund National Labor Relations Board; favor right-to-work

Q: New Hampshire could soon become the 23rd state to pass right to work legislation. Unions don't like it because it makes membership voluntary. Would you support a federal right-to-work law?

A: One of the things the Congress should do immediately is defund the National Labor Relations Board which has gone into South Carolina to punish Boeing, which wants to put 8,000 American jobs in S.C. by fundamentally eliminating right-to-work at the National Labor Relations Board. That's a real, immediate threat from the Obama administration to eliminate right to work. And I think that it is fundamentally the wrong direction.

I hope that New Hampshire does adopt right-to-work. I frankly keep it at the state level because as each new state becomes right to work, they send a signal to the remaining states, don't be stupid. If you believe in the 10th Amendment, we ought to let the states learn from each other. And the right-to-work states are creating a lot more jobs today that they heavily unionized states.

Source: 2011 GOP primary debate in Manchester NH, June 13, 2011

Santorum on Offshore Jobs

Offshore jobs return
if you repeal manufacturing regulations

Q: You've said that when you were growing up in a PA steel town, 21% of the country was involved in manufacturing. Now it's down to 9%. Can those jobs ever return?

SANTORUM: Yeah, the jobs can come back if you create a climate for them to be profitable We have a lot of manufacturers in Pennsylvania. I don't know a single one who wanted to ship their jobs offshore, who didn't want them in their own community to be able to employ people and see the fruits of their labor benefiting the community that they live in. What happened was we became uncompetitive. So we need to be competitive.

And that's why I proposed taking the corporate tax from 35% and eliminating it, zero percent tax. Allow this to be the manufacturing capital of the world again. Repeal every regulation the Obama administration has put in place that's over $100 million. Repeal them all. You may have to replace a few, but let's repeal them all because they are all antagonistic to businesses, particularly in the manufacturing sector.

Source: GOP debate at Dartmouth College, NH, Oct. 11, 2011

Gingrich on Offshore Jobs

2002 Sarbanes-Oxley Act drives IPOs out of the US

A 2005 press report by the London Stock Exchange attributed one reason for its success to the fact that "about 38% of the international companies surveyed said they had considered the US. Of those, 90% said the onerous demands of the new Sarbanes-Oxley corporate governance law had made London listing more attractive."

The 2002 Sarbanes-Oxley Act, which added massive new reams of accounting red tape for businesses, has driven IPOs out of the US. Furthermore, the legislation is leading public companies to delist from the stock market in order to avoid red tape (and potential criminal penalties). The Sarbanes-Oxley Act effectively drives businesses to be *less* accountable than they were before and has done vastly more damage to the American economy than the corporate accounting scandals it was supposed to reform. It has had a substantial effect on New York as a financial center and has been a big asset for London. It is a wound inflicted by Congress on the American economy.

Source: Real Change, by Newt Gingrich, pp.136-8, Dec. 18, 2007

NOTES: "IPO" means "Initial Public Offering," describing when a company first offers stock to the public on a stock exchange. "Sarbanes-Oxley" refers to the Corporate and Auditing Accountability and Responsibility Act, named after its sponsors, Sen. Paul Sarbanes (D, MD) and Rep. Michael Oxley (R, OH). Sarbanes-Oxley standardized accounting practices to avoid false reporting of corporate profits. In response to corporate accounting scandals, the law passed Congress with an overwhelming bipartisan majority, and was signed into law by Pres. Bush in 2002.

Santorum on Social Security Privatization

Supports privatization if voluntary

Q: Will you support or oppose using Social Security taxes to fund private accounts?

A: I only support using Social Security taxes to fund private accounts if such an option is voluntary. I believe that Social Security must remain a program that our children & grandchildren can depend on—we owe it to them to provide for their retirement security as they have provided for current and previous generations. As proposals for strengthening this valuable system for future retirees are considered, I believe that all options should remain on the table. I take seriously my responsibility of working to protect current and near retirees, while ensuring sustainable financial security and peace of mind for future generations.

Source: AARP Senate candidate questionnaire, Sept. 29, 2006

No privatization; but personal retirement accounts

My colleagues will not hear me use the term "privatization." Privatization intimates to the American public that we are going to abandon the current Social Security system and turn it over to completely private accounts. What every bill over on this side of the aisle proposes is to take a portion of the contribution that comes into the Social Security Administration and give people the option voluntarily to establish a personal retirement account to be part of their Social Security benefit which continues to be guaranteed as much as it is under current law. We have proposed a solution that uses the power of the market, which uses individual choice.

Source: Santorum speech in "A Senator Speaks Out," p. 71, Sept. 22, 2003

Gingrich on Social Security Privatization

Take Social Security off federal budget; give young a choice

You deal with Social Security as a free-standing issue. And the fact is, if you allow younger Americans to have the choice to go to a Galveston or Chilean-style personal Social Security savings account, the long-term effect on Social Security is scored by the Social Security actuary as absolutely stabilizing the system and taking care of it.

The key is there is $2.4 trillion in Social Security which should be off budget, and no president of the United States should ever again say because of some political fight in Washington, I may not be able to send you your check. That money is sitting there. That money is available. And the country ought to pay the debt it owes the people who put the money in there.

Source: 2011 CNBC GOP Primary debate in Rochester Michigan,
Nov. 9, 2011

Santorum on Retirement Age

Raise retirement age? Maybe. Private investment? Yes

Senator Santorum, on a videotape made in 1994, said he planned to raise the retirement age for Social Security benefits and to privatize the program. Santorum says he believes that Social Security should not be paid out until workers hit the age of 70. "It is ridiculous that we have a retirement age in this country of age 65 today," Santorum says emphatically, noting that many people receive benefits for two decades before dying. "Push it back to at least age 70," continues the senator. "I'd go even further if I could, but I don't think I could pass it." Santorum has since backed away from raising the retirement age, but he's in the forefront of pushing for younger workers to be allowed to invest part of their payroll taxes themselves.

Source: Jill Zuckman, Boston Globe, p. A1 & A12, May 15, 2000

1994: Proposed raising retirement age, despite unpopularity

I was out in 1994 running against a Democratic incumbent, and I went out and talked about Social Security reform. Why? Because I knew this day was coming. And I had the courage to go out and say Social Security is in trouble. And I told a group of young people at La Salle University that we needed to do something like raising the retirement age. They ran that on TV for 3 weeks prior to the election. And I still won the election. Why? Because the people of Pennsylvania wanted someone who had the courage to tell them the truth. And I had the courage to tell them the truth.

Source: Tea Party debate in Tampa FL, Sept. 12, 2011

Gingrich on Retirement Age

Take away politicians' power & control
over our retirement

Q: Would you raise the retirement age for Social Security recipients?

GINGRICH: No, not necessarily.

Q: What would you do to fix Social Security?

GINGRICH: President Obama twice said recently he couldn't guarantee delivering the checks to Social Security recipients. Now, why should young people who are 16 to 25 years old have politicians have the power for the rest of their life to threaten to take away their Social Security? Now, I just want to make two simple points about Social Security and how you save it. The first is, you get back to a full employment economy. The second is, everybody who is older and wants to be totally protected, fine, no change. But if you're younger and you would like a personal account, you would control instead of the politicians. And you know you'll have more money at the end of your lifetime if you control it than the politicians. Why shouldn't you have the right?

Source: Tea Party debate in Tampa FL, Sept. 12, 2011

Santorum on Death Tax

Changing estate tax would cost $100B, not save $730B

Q: How would you get a balanced budget?

CASEY: When it comes to the budget, what's missing principally is a lack of fiscal responsibility. [We should] repeal the tax cut for people making over $200,000 a year. That change, in addition to an estate tax change, could get you about $730 billion over 10 years.

Q: How does that balance the current budget?

CASEY: You can't balance a budget in one year. They've put us in such a fiscal hole, it will take many years.

Q: Well, give me a couple ideas.

SANTORUM: Changing the estate tax cut would cost money over the long term, not save money. The death tax snaps back to the old death tax in 2011, and it would cost $100 million just to do the changes that he suggested. I'm for not taking more people's money when they die.

Source: PA Senate Debate, Tim Russert moderator, Sept. 3, 2006

Gingrich on Death Tax

Death tax is a direct assault on civil society

Expansive government rapidly becomes expensive government, and that requires new and higher taxes. The transfer of money from citizens to the bureaucracy then further weakens civil society & leads to even more expensive & even more expensive government. That effort to finance Big Government through higher taxes is a direct assault on civil society, and the "death tax" is a prime example. This tax, which is in a constant state of flux and was resurrected in 2001 after effectively disappearing in 2010, falls especially hard on small business. That sector contributes immensely to America's social and economic dynamism, often acting as the cornerstone of community organizations and local philanthropy. Entrepreneurs and shopkeepers are community leaders and, when prosperous, are generous with their time and money. Prosperity and generosity are highly correlated, as those with more to give feel obliged to give more.

Source: A Nation Like No Other, by Newt Gingrich, pp.129-30,
Jun 13, 2011

Repeal tax hikes in capital gains and death taxes

Gingrich signed the Contract From America, clause 10:

Stop the Tax Hikes: Permanently repeal all tax hikes, including those to the income, capital gains, and death taxes, currently scheduled to begin in 2011.

Source: The Contract From America on July 8, 2010

Santorum on Tax Simplification

Simplify tax code: just 5 deductions; everything else goes

HUNTSMAN: I would have done what Simpson-Bowles recommended. I would have cleaned out all of the loopholes and the deductions that weigh down this country to the tune of $1.1 trillion.

Q: [to Santorum]: How would you raise the kind of revenues called for in the Simpson-Bowles Commission?

SANTORUM: Our plan puts together a package that focuses on simplifying the tax code and I agree with Gov. Huntsman on that. Five deductions: Health care, housing, pensions, children and charities. Everything else goes. We focus on the pillars that have broad consensus of this country in the important sectors of our economy, including our children. The other side is the corporate side. Cut it in half, to 17.5%. But I do something different than anybody else. I'm very worried about a sector of our economy that has been under fire. I come from southwestern Pennsylvania, the heart of the steel country, the heart of manufacturing. And it's been devastated because we are uncompetitive.

Source: WMUR 2012 GOP New Hampshire debate, Jan. 7, 2012

NOTE: "Simpson-Bowles" refers to the National Commission on Fiscal Responsibility and Reform, and its conclusions released in 2010. It is named after its two chairs, Sen. Alan Simpson (R, WY) and Erskine Bowles (D, NC). The Commission proposed reducing the national debt by a combination of increased revenue (raising taxes, including a 15-cent gas tax); reductions in discretionary spending; Medicare cost controls; raising the Social Security retirement age; and a reduction in entitlements.

Gingrich on Tax Simplification

Adopt a single-rate tax system

Gingrich signed the Contract From America, clause 4:

Enact Fundamental Tax Reform: Adopt a simple and fair single-rate tax system by scrapping the internal revenue code and replacing it with one that is no longer than 4,543 words—the length of the original Constitution.

Source: The Contract From America on July 8, 2010

Flat tax proposal criticized for losing popular tax breaks

Four out of five Americans would like to have the option of a one-page tax form with a single tax rate. This concept of an optional flat tax rate was developed by Steve Forbes when his flat tax campaign was undermined by criticisms that it would take away popular tax breaks. Forbes proposed giving American taxpayers an opportunity to choose simplicity versus complexity and a single rate over a lot of deductions. They call it the free choice flat tax, and it's an idea whose time has come.

All workers and corporations would have the freedom to choose each year to file their income taxes either under the new free choice flat tax option or under the current US income tax code.

Rhode Island adopted an optional flat tax, and lawmakers there expect that it will make the state more competitive with neighboring states in attracting new business and entrepreneurs who create jobs.

Source: Real Change, by Newt Gingrich, p.143-144, Dec. 18, 2007

Santorum on Corporation Policy

Cut all corporate tax rates to zero

What we need is a pro-growth plan that can pass the Congress with Democratic support and be able to rally the American people. What the American people want is a policy that's going to get people the opportunity to rise in society, to fill that great middle of America, and that is manufacturing jobs.

That's why my plan takes the corporate tax, which is 35%, cuts it to zero, and says, if you manufacture in America, you aren't going to pay any taxes. We want you to come back here.

Source: Tea Party debate in Tampa FL, Sept. 12, 2011

Cut the corporate tax to zero, to create jobs

We cut the corporate tax from 35% to zero, because we want to build the great middle of America again, get those jobs that were shipped overseas by companies that were looking too make a profit because they couldn't any longer do it here, and bring those jobs back to America. We pass repatriation to get those resources that are overseas, $1.2 trillion, and we bring them back here.

We'll create jobs, and I'll get Democratic votes to pass it. We'll bring things together, because those industrial state Democrats—and I know, because I'm from an industrial state—they will vote for this bill. You want to get something going, elect someone who knows how to get things done.

Source: GOP debate in Simi Valley CA at the Reagan Library, Sept. 7, 2011

Gingrich on Corporation Policy

Businesses focus on customers; apply Lean Six Sigma to government

CAIN: You spent a lot of distinguished years in Congress and then you left Congress and started other ventures and you were thinking outside the Washington bubble. What are three things you realized outside that bubble?

GINGRICH: As a business, you don't get to stay in business unless you wake up every day thinking about how to keep customers. If you don't earn your pay in business, a business won't pay you. We need to apply Lean Six Sigma principles to government. In every aspect of the private sector someone is doing something brilliant that could be applied to government to reduce costs, but the Left and the media block this. If you found Best Practices across the country, you would be amazed at how quickly you could balance the budget and resolve the deficit. When I left office as Speaker, there was a swing of $5 *trillion* and we had a balanced budget. CEOs set big goals with tight deadlines, delegate smartly, and don't let any so-called experts in the room.

Source: Head-to-head debate between Herman Cain & Newt Gingrich, Nov 5, 2011

NOTE: "Six Sigma" refers to a business management strategy developed by Edwards Deming in the 1980s, based on a cycle of "Plan-Do-Check-Act." The complementary "lean manufacturing" methods focus on process and waste (making work faster), where Six Sigma focuses on design (making work better). In recent years, the combined strategy has become known as "Lean Six Sigma."

Santorum vs. Gingrich on Social Issues

Social issues focus on matters which are based primarily on moral values, including the following topics:

- *Abortion:* including stem cells, partial birth, and state-level restrictions. This topic has always been the most viewed topic on our websitewww.OnTheIssues.org, so we explore several aspects. Santorum and Gingrich both oppose abortion on moral grounds.

- *Civil Rights:* including gay rights and minority rights. For the 2012 race, gay rights will dominate this category. Both candidates would ban same-sex marriage nationally. Sen. Santorum is surprisingly supportive of affirmative action; he just doesn't talk about it much on the campaign trail.

- *Education:* including college funding issues, school vouchers, and school prayer. Santorum and Gingrich share the traditional conservative stances supporting vouchers, homeschooling, and exposure to religious values in public schools.

- *Families and Children:* including father's rights and family values. Not a key focus for Speaker Gingrich, but the focus of Santorum's book *It Takes a Family*; his views on the centrality of family to American culture permeate many other issues.

- *Principles and Values:* including religious issues, on which Gingrich has written a book, *Rediscovering God in America.* This category includes the candidates' definitions of conservatism and of the Tea Party.

- *Welfare and Poverty:* including homelessness, welfare payments, and other poverty programs. Santorum and Gingrich collaborated in the 1990s to pass the landmark welfare reform bill; obviously, they agree on this issue: limit welfare benefits and focus on getting welfare recipients to work.

Rick Santorum
on Social Issues

Santorum on Birth Control: 78
   States have the right to ban contraception, but shouldn't

Santorum on Abortion Funding: 80
   FactCheck: Under 1/4 of pregnancies end in abortion, not 1/3

Santorum on Abortion Morality: 82
   Scientifically, embryo is human from moment of conception

Santorum on Welfare State: 84
   Poverty is not a disability; believe in ability to work

Santorum on Welfare in Contract With America: 86
   Drafted 1994 Contract with America Welfare Reform

Santorum on Don't-Ask-Don't-Tell: 88
   Repeal Don't-Ask-Don't-Tell; punish behavior

Santorum on Defense of Marriage Act: 90
   Marriage is a federal issue; we need one definition, not 50

Santorum on Churches and Same-Sex Marriage: 92
   Right to gay sex implies right to bigamy, incest, & adultery

Santorum on Affirmative Action: 94
   Affirmative program for minority business-building

Santorum on Homeschooling: 96
   Home-schooled six children with wife Karen

Santorum on School Vouchers: 98
   Rich people already have school choice; give it to the poor

Santorum on Religion in Schools: 100
   Expose kids to legitimate debate of evolution & creationism

Santorum on Church-State Separation: 102
   Church-state "neutrality" is not in US Constitution

Santorum on American Faith: 104
   Govern via both faith & reason

Santorum on the Tea Party: 106
   Tea Party is now the backbone of conservative movement

Santorum on Conservative Values: 108
   I'm a conservative but not a libertarian; some government OK

Newt Gingrich
on Social Issues

Gingrich on Birth Control: 79
    Reward high-school girls who graduate as virgins

Gingrich on Abortion Funding: 81
    Immediately cease public funding for abortion providers

Gingrich on Abortion Morality: 83
    Stop forcing pro-choice morality on religious organizations

Gingrich on Welfare State: 85
    When free welfare is provided, people choose not to work

Gingrich on Welfare in Contract With America: 87
    Welfare vouchers allow choice & reduce bureaucracy

Gingrich on Don't-Ask-Don't-Tell: 89
    Army & Marines wanted Don't-Ask-Don't-Tell

Gingrich on Defense of Marriage Act: 91
    I helped author DOMA; if it fails, amend Constitution

Gingrich on Churches and Same-Sex Marriage: 93
    Stop forcing same-sex marriage on religious organizations

Gingrich on Affirmative Action: 95
    Affirmative action OK individually, but not by group

Gingrich on Homeschooling: 97
    Let parents choose public, private, parochial, or homeschool

Gingrich on School Vouchers: 99
    Voucherize inner-city programs from schools to groceries

Gingrich on Religion in Schools: 101
    Voluntary school prayer creates bond between you & Creator

Gingrich on Church-State Separation: 103
    Declaration assumes God created man

Gingrich on American Faith: 105
    Five habits of liberty sustain American Exceptionalism

Gingrich on the Tea Party: 107
    Tea Party prevents mistake of electing conservative Dems

Gingrich on Conservative Values: 109
    Liberals exploit weakness; conservatives offer strength

Santorum on Birth Control

States have the right to ban contraception, but shouldn't

Q: [to Romney] Sen. Santorum has been very clear in his belief that the Supreme Court was wrong when it decided that a right to privacy was embedded in the Constitution. And following from that, he believes that states have the right to ban contraception. Now I should add that he said he's not recommending that states do that.

SANTORUM: No, let's be clear. We're talking about the 10th Amendment and the right of states to act.

Q: Gov. Romney, do you believe that states have the right to ban contraception? Or is that trumped by a constitutional right to privacy?

ROMNEY: I can't imagine a state banning contraception. I would totally and completely oppose any effort to ban contraception.

SANTORUM: The Supreme Court created through a penumbra of rights a new right to privacy that was not in the Constitution. It created a right through boot-strapping, through creating something that wasn't there. I believe it should be overturned.

Source: WMUR 2012 GOP New Hampshire debate, Jan. 7, 2012

Gingrich on Birth Control

Reward high-school girls who graduate as virgins

As part of his conservative stance, Newt Gingrich aims to impose order with a vision like a surreal projection of his own past; a family structure as strict as [his father] Bob Gingrich's military hierarchy and an educational system that, as he outlines for me, rewards high-school girls who graduate as virgins.

In his book *To Renew America*, he suggests that one could communicate values to children by simply getting out "the Boy Scout or Girl Scout handbook, or go look at *Reader's Digest* and *The Saturday Evening Post* from around 1955." In his dream of perfection, as marketable and soothing as "Father of the Bride," there are none of the ordinary dramas of family life.

Source: PBS Frontline: "The Inner Quest of Newt Gingrich," Nov. 11, 2011

Santorum on Abortion Funding

FactCheck: Under 1/4 of pregnancies end in abortion, not 1/3

Santorum wrongly claimed that "one in three pregnancies end in abortion" in the US when saying that abortion was to blame for funding problems for Social Security and Medicare. Santorum said: "The reason Social Security is in big trouble is we don't have enough workers to support the retirees. Well, a third of all the young people in America are not in America today because of abortion, because one in three pregnancies end in abortion."

First, fewer than one in four pregnancies ended in abortion in 2008, the most recent statistics available. Second, Santorum assumes the population is lower by a number equal to total abortions, but that's not the case. One analyst told us "most women obtain abortions to postpone childbearing not to prevent it altogether" and an unknown number of pregnancies would have ended in miscarriage.

Source: FactCheck.org on 2011 GOP primary debate in South Carolina, May 6, 2011

Voted YES on maintaining ban on Military Base Abortions

Vote on a motion to table [kill] an amendment that would repeal the ban on privately funded abortions at overseas military facilities.

Source: Bill S 2549 ; vote number 134 on June 20, 2000

Gingrich on Abortion Funding

Immediately cease public funding for abortion providers

Abortion is perhaps the most contentious public issue today, testing the professed American principle that every human life is precious and entitled to constitutional protection. With the advent of increasingly sophisticated ultrasound technology, public opinion on abortion has shifted, with a majority of Americans now identifying themselves as pro-life. As with any public policy, the more strongly public opinion is swayed in defense of unborn life, the more our laws should and will change as a result.

Source: A Nation Like No Other, by Newt Gingrich, p. 92, June 13, 2011

Santorum on Abortion Morality

Scientifically, an embryo is human from moment of conception

I was very much like most Americans and most nominal Catholics before I decided to enter public life. I didn't like the idea of abortion—I knew it was wrong, but I wasn't sure if it was the government's business to do anything about it. When I decided to run for public office in 1989, I was told that I had to "make up my mind on abortion."

Through both scientific reasoning and moral reasoning the answer was clear to me. Abortion was the taking of an innocent human life. Scientifically, the embryo is human from the moment of conception (it has a complete, unique human genetic code) and it is alive: therefore, it is literally a human life.

I looked at it one other way. Did I see the child in the womb as a person entitled to protection under the law, or as a property owned by the mother, with no rights until the moment she was physically separated from her mother? No, I couldn't see myself on the "mere property" side of this argument.

Source: It Takes a Family, by Sen. Rick Santorum, p.239-40,
Apr 30, 2006

Gingrich on Abortion Morality

Stop forcing pro-choice morality
on religious organizations

The campaign against public prayer and the display of religious symbols is only the tip of the iceberg. Consider the following examples:

- In May 2009, a pro-life nurse at a New York hospital was forced to participate in a late-term abortion, even though the hospital had agreed in writing to honor her religious convictions.

- In Jan. 2010, a Baptist minister was sentenced to thirty days in jail for peacefully protesting outside a Planned Parenthood abortion clinic in Oakland, California.

- In Feb. 2010, five men were threatened with arrest for preaching Christianity on a public sidewalk in Virginia.

The Founders would have regarded such efforts to remove God from public life as a fundamental threat to liberty. They saw no contradiction between the First Amendment, which was designed to PROTECT religious liberty, and the need for a free people to remember that their liberties come from God.

Source: A Nation Like No Other, by Newt Gingrich, p. 87-89,
June 13, 2011

Santorum on Welfare State

Poverty is not a disability; believe in ability to work

Look at welfare reform. I remember standing next to Sens. Pat Moynihan & Ted Kennedy, who were talking about how this was going to be the end of civilization; there would be bread lines; the horrific consequences of removing federal income support from mothers with children.

And we stood up and said, no, that creating that dependency upon federal dollars is more harmful than not believing in people and their ability to work. And so we stood up and fought, and went out to the American public. Bill Clinton vetoed this bill twice. We had hard opposition, but I was able to work together and paint a vision.

We made compromises, but not on our core principles. The core principles were: this was going to end a federal program; we were going to require work; we were going to put time limits on welfare. I stuck to those principles, and we were able to compromise on some things like transportation funding and some day care funding, all in order to get a consensus that poverty is not a disability.

Source: Meet the Press 2012 GOP New Hampshire debate, Jan. 8, 2012

Gingrich on Welfare State

When free welfare is provided, people choose not to work

President Lyndon Johnson famously announced the War on Poverty. From 1965 to 2008, total spending on this "war" reached nearly $16 trillion in 2008 dollars. And what did we get in return? Soon after the War on Poverty programs were adopted, the years-long decline in American poverty suddenly stopped.

By 2009 the poverty rate stood at 14.3%—about where it was when the War of Poverty began. With the government providing so much in free welfare, many people chose not to work. Welfare recipients who go to work lose their benefits as their income rises. This is effectively an extra tax on work that must be paid on top of the usual array of federal, state, and local taxes.

Source: A Nation Like No Other, by Newt Gingrich, p.109, June 13, 2011

FactCheck: Poverty rate has fallen under War on Poverty

PolitiFact.com reports: [LBJ's programs] focused on elderly poverty, which is down to 13%. [Gingrich also] uses the wrong numbers. The poverty rate was 17.3% in 1965, not 14%. So the poverty has fallen by 3 percentage points, or by about 1/6 its original level. Counting different years shows even more decline. In 1962, the poverty rate ranged was 20%. In pre-recession 2007, it stood at 12.5%. Comparing 1962 and 2007, the poverty rate dropped by over 1/3.

Source: FactCheck by PolitiFact.com, July 26, 2011

Santorum on Welfare in Contract With America

Drafted & managed 1994
Contract with America Welfare Reform

Q: I'm not a libertarian Republican, I'm not a Tea Party Republican. I'm just a mainstream Republican. How can you convince me you won't be torn to one side or the other for many factions within the party?

SANTORUM: If you look at my record, I'm someone who's actually accomplished a lot on big issues. Take for example, welfare reform. I drafted the Contract with America Welfare Reform Bill. It was considered this extreme measure. But I managed that bill and we ended up winning. I didn't believe that poverty was the ultimate disability. I believed that people could work and they could succeed. And we brought people together. I got 70 votes [out of 100 in the Senate] to end a federal entitlement. I led and got bipartisan support to do it.

Source: GOP primary debate in Manchester NH, June 13, 2011

Support time-limits for able-bodied welfare recipients

Bill Clinton promised in 1992 to "end welfare as we know it." But by late 1993, he had all but shelved his plan to reform welfare. Our Minority Whip Newt Gingrich asked me to get together a group of members to draft our own welfare reform bill. The bill we drafted was an integral part of the now famous Contract with America. We wanted to require able-bodied welfare recipients to work or else lose their benefits.

Source: It Takes a Family, by Rick Santorum, pp.131–4, April 30, 2006

Gingrich on Welfare in Contract With America

Welfare vouchers allow choice & reduce bureaucracy

In Gingrich's 1984 book *Window of Opportunity*, welfare programs received a scant three pages. Gingrich proposed that recipients receive cash and credit card vouchers directly in order to allow more choices and, not coincidentally, chip away at the bureaucracy. It was a precursor of the plank in the Contract With America to turn programs into block grants for the states.

In 1984, Gingrich urged the creation of day care centers for welfare mothers who would be forced to leave home to work or study. But in another preview of the Contract With America, Gingrich suggested that minor girls should be ineligible for Aid to Families With Dependent Children if they became pregnant. Aid would go first to their parents or guardians.

Source: Newt!, by Dick Williams, p. 39, June 1, 1995

Limit welfare to 2 years & cut welfare spending

Gingrich wrote the Contract with America: [Within 100 days we pledge to bring to the House Floor the following bill]:

The Personal Responsibility Act: Discourage illegitimacy and teen pregnancy by prohibiting welfare to minor mothers and denying increased AFDC for additional children while on welfare, cut spending for welfare programs, and enact a tough two-years-and-out provision with work requirements to promote individual responsibility.

Source: Contract with America on Sept. 27, 1994

Santorum on Don't-Ask-Don't-Tell

Repeal Don't-Ask-Don't-Tell; punish behavior

Q: Now gays are allowed to serve openly in the military; would you leave that policy in place or would you try to change it back to "don't ask/don't tell"?

PAUL: I would not work to overthrow it. We have to remember, rights don't come in groups. We shouldn't have gay rights. Rights come as individuals. If we have this major debate going on, it would be behavior that would count, not the person who belongs to which group.

SANTORUM: The job of the United States military is to protect and defend the people of this country. It is not for social experimentation. It should be repealed. And the commanders should have a system of discipline in place, as Ron Paul said, that punishes bad behavior.

Source: GOP primary debate in Manchester NH, June 13, 2011

NOTE: The policy banning open homosexuals serving in the military was repealed on Sept. 20, 2011. Hence gay and lesbian people may now openly serve in the US military. Since 1993, the DADT policy held that homosexuals may serve as long as they do not announce their homosexuality ("Don't Tell"), but also that the military may not investigate their homosexuality ("Don't Ask").

Gingrich on Don't-Ask-Don't-Tell

Army & Marines wanted Don't-Ask-Don't-Tell

Q: Now gays are allowed to serve openly in the military; would you leave that policy in place or would you try to change it back to "don't ask/don't tell"?

CAIN: If I had my druthers, I never would have overturned "don't ask/don't tell" in the first place. Now that they have changed it, I wouldn't create a distraction trying to turn it over as president.

GINGRICH: Well, I think it's very powerful that both the Army and the Marines overwhelmingly opposed changing it, that their recommendation was against changing it. And if as president—I've met with them and they said, you know, it isn't working, it is dangerous, it's disrupting unit morale, and we should go back, I would listen to the commanders whose lives are at risk about the young men and women that they are, in fact, trying to protect.

BACHMANN: I would keep the "don't ask/don't tell" policy.

Source: GOP primary debate in Manchester NH, June 13, 2011

Santorum on Defense of Marriage Act

Marriage is a federal issue;
we need one definition, not 50

Q: Your view on the 1,800 couples who have same-sex marriages under N.H. law?

SANTORUM: I believe the issue of marriage is a federal issue, that we can't have different laws with respect to marriage. We have to have one law. Marriage is a foundational institution of our country, and we have to have a singular law with respect to that. We can't have somebody married in one state and not married in another.

Q: If we have a federal constitutional amendment banning same-sex marriage, what happens to the 1,800 families who have married here in N.H.? Are their marriages basically illegitimate at this point?

SANTORUM: If the Constitution says marriage is between a man and a woman, then marriage is between a man and a woman. And therefore, that's what marriage is and would be in this country. And those who are not men and women who are married—would not be married. That's what the Constitution would say.

Source: WMUR 2012 GOP New Hampshire debate, Jan. 7, 2012

NOTE: As of Jan. 2012, the current status of state laws regarding same-sex marriage:

- 6 states allow same-sex marriage:
  CT, DC, IA, MA, NH, NY, VT.

- 13 states allow same-sex civil unions or similar legislation:
  CA, CO, DE, HI, IL, MD, ME, NJ, NV, OR, RI, WA, WI.

- 29 states have laws defining marriage as one-man-one-woman.

Gingrich on Defense of Marriage Act

I helped author DOMA; if it fails, amend Constitution

Q: Are you a George W. Bush Republican, meaning a constitutional amendment to ban same-sex marriage, or a Dick Cheney Republican, that same sex marriage should be a state's decision?

GINGRICH: I helped author the Defense of Marriage Act which the Obama administration should be protecting in court. I think if that fails, you have no choice except a constitutional amendment.

SANTORUM: Constitutional amendment.

PAWLENTY: Constitutional amendment.

CAIN: State decision.

ROMNEY: Constitutional.

Source: 2011 GOP primary debate in Manchester NH, June 13, 2011

NOTE: "DOMA" refers to the Defense of Marriage Act, passed by Congress in 1996, which defined marriage as consisting of one man and one woman (in other words, barring same-sex marriage). DOMA applies to all federal benefits and taxes, but not necessarily to state benefits and taxes.

Santorum on Churches and Same-Sex Marriage

Right to gay sex implies right to bigamy, incest, & adultery

Quote: "Is anyone saying same-sex couples can't love each other? I love my children. I love my friends, my brother. Heck, I even love my mother-in-law. Should we call these relationships marriage, too?" (Santorum's Philadelphia Inquirer column, May 22, 2008)

Quote: "If the Supreme Court says that you have the right to consensual [gay] sex within your home, then you have the right to bigamy, you have the right to polygamy, you have the right to incest, you have the right to adultery. You have the right to anything. Does that undermine the fabric of our society? I would argue yes, it does. That's not to pick on homosexuality. It's not man on child, or man on dog, or whatever the case may be." (AP interview, April 7, 2003)

Reaction: "Rick Santorum has expended a great deal of thought and energy to finding new words to disparage gay marriage," says an analyst at Breaking Copy. But even if you agree with Santorum, "would you really want a president who is this obsessed" with gay sex?

Source: Santorum's "9 most controversial statements" in The Week,
Jan. 5, 2012

Gingrich on Churches and Same-Sex Marriage

Stop forcing same-sex marriage on religious organizations

The campaign against religious symbols is only the tip of the iceberg. Consider the following:

In Nov. 2006, a student at Missouri State University studying to be a social worker was interrogated by school faculty and subsequently threatened with expulsion when, after being required to lobby state legislators in favor of same-sex adoptions, she asked for an alternative assignment that did not violate her Christian beliefs.

In Oct. 2009, Congress passed a "hate speech" law subjecting pastors and other faith leaders to prosecution for preaching aspects of their faith that the state decides are "hate speech."

A Methodist camp meeting association in New Jersey now faces civil rights charges after refusing now faces civil rights charges after refusing a request to host a same-sex couple's "civil union ceremony" in its worship space.

A young Christian photographer was fined nearly $7,000 in attorney's fees after she refused to photograph the "commitment ceremony" of a same-sex couple.

Source: A Nation Like No Other, by Newt Gingrich, pp. 87-8,
June 13, 2011

Santorum on Affirmative Action

Affirmative program for minority business-building

Our nation's African-Americans were most assuredly victims in countless ways. Obviously, racism and discrimination still do exist in this country.

But it is wrong to believe the African-American story is one of victimhood only. To think in those terms is to deny the real accomplishments of the black community in our history, [especially] a tradition of business acumen and entrepreneurship.

There remains a very troubling disparity between whites and blacks. And this is really the result of a missing economic fundamental: business building and wealth creation.

Surely the most *affirmative* program to build up America's minority families would be one aimed at just this: using market-based solutions and public-private partnership emphasizing *business creation*. We need to hang up "No Denials" signs in urban communities—the opposite of red-lining.

Source: It Takes a Family, by Rick Santorum, pp.189-92, April 30, 2006

Voted NO on banning affirmative action hiring with federal funds

Vote to disallow any funds in the Legislative Appropriations bill from being used to award, require, or encourage any Federal contract, if the contract is being awarded on the basis of the race, color, national origin, or gender of the contractor.

Source: Bill HR 1854 ; vote number 317 on July 20, 1995

Gingrich on Affirmative Action

Affirmative action OK individually, but not by group

In 1995, a California referendum [was proposed to] eliminate affirmative action programs in state and local government. When Gingrich was asked about the issue at his regular daily press conference, he was consistent.

"It is my belief," he said, "that affirmative action programs, if done for individuals, are good, and if done by some group distinction, are bad. Because it is antithetical to the American dream to measure people by the genetic pattern of their great-grandmothers. So, I'm very interested in rewriting the affirmative action programs so that they allow individuals to get help whether they are Appalachian white or blacks from Atlanta. But I think it ought to be based on the fact that you individually have worked hard and are trying to rise and that you come out of a background of poverty and a background of cultural need."

A reporter noted that some beneficiaries of government preferences have been subjected to discrimination for centuries. "That's been true of virtually every American."

Source: Newt!, by Dick Williams, p. 31, June 1, 1995

Santorum on Homeschooling

Home-schooled six children with wife Karen

My wife and I [decided that our] six children should be home-schooled. My wife Karen is trained as a nurse and a lawyer, and our kids are lucky to have such a talented person as their primary educator. (Yes, I help out too, but for most families it makes sense for one parent to take on the primary educational role.) However, research suggests that there is no correlation between educational level of parents and the educational success of their homeschooled children.

We didn't set out with any grand plan for homeschooling. It just happened rather naturally, when we couldn't find a kindergarten for our oldest child that we were happy with. Eventually, we took the same approach with all our children. But we did it one year at a time, each year making a decision as to what was the best course for each child.

The greatest thing about homeschooling is that, though it's hard and stressful at times, you develop this amazingly close relationship with your kids.

Source: It Takes a Family, by Rick Santorum, p.384, April 30, 2006

Gingrich on Homeschooling

Let parents choose public, private, parochial, or homeschool

Home-educated students score an average of 15 to 30 points higher than public-school students on standardized tests, including the SAT and ACT, regardless of their parents' level of formal education or the level of family income. Because families who homeschool do not depend on taxpayer-funded resources, taxpayers save an estimated $16 billion each year thanks to homeschooling.

Except in cases of demonstrable neglect or abuse, lawmakers and judges must enact and enforce policies that support the right of parents to direct the upbringing of their children and choose the educational model that best suits the child's needs, whether public school, private or parochial school, or homeschooling.

Source: A Nation Like No Other, by Newt Gingrich, pp. 94-5,
June 13, 2011

Santorum on School Vouchers

Rich people already have school choice; give it to the poor

We already have school choice in this country. The problem is that we've only got school choice for people who can afford it.

School choice today takes two forms. The most obvious form is the choice exercised by those who can afford to pay the cost of private school. Second, there's an affordable from of school choice, which happens every day in every community in America. It's called *moving*.

We've got residential school choice already. The same hysterical criticisms apply: It creams off the best students! More resources go to school that are already better!

So we have plenty of school choice today already. But it's inefficient and unfair. It's disruptive and costly to move. And it's inequitable. Low-income families can't move, so they are stuck; their children are stuck. We must empower *all* our children with scholarships if we are to achieve common good.

Source: It Takes a Family, by Rick Santorum, pp.365-6, April 30, 2006

Voted YES on school vouchers in DC

This legislation would have amended the DC spending measure, imposing an unconstitutional school voucher program on the District. Status: Cloture Motion Rejected, 58-41

Source: DC Appropriations Act; Bill S. 1156 ;
vote number 260 on Sept. 30, 1997

Gingrich on School Vouchers

Voucherize inner-city programs from schools to groceries

In a speech in March, 1995, to business leaders in suburban Atlanta, Gingrich noted that the public school system in the District of Columbia spends $9,600 a year per pupil, nearly double the national average. He suggested that for such a high level of spending, each could have private tutors and personal transportation to school—plus lunch. He advocates vouchers to parents so they can choose the schools, public or private, their children will attend.

"I think we ought to voucherize every program in the inner city with cash payments to parents allowing them to decide where and what to purchase, be it an elementary school, health care, or groceries." Some in his audience thought he was exaggerating to make a point. In a later interview, he was willing to go even further. "Suppose you need to get children away from failed teachers. What if we called on the home-schoolers in Maryland and Virginia to come to D.C. for a massive home schooling program, teaching parents how to teach their children."

Source: Newt!, by Dick Williams, pp. 51-2, June 1, 1995

Santorum on Religion in Schools

Expose kids to legitimate debate of evolution & creationism

Some evolution opponents are trying to use Bush's No Child Left Behind law. Santorum drafted language accompanying the law that said students should be exposed to "the full range of scientific views that exist": "Anyone who expresses anything other than the dominant worldview is shunned and booted from the academy," Santorum said in an interview. "My reading of the science is there's a legitimate debate. My feeling is let the debate be had."

Source: Peter Slevin in Washington Post, p. A1, March 14, 2005

Teach about disagreements in evolution theories

This amendment is simply two sentences—it simply says there are disagreements in scientific theories out there that are continually tested:

1. Good science education should prepare students to distinguish the data or testable theories of science from philosophical or religious claims that are made in the name of science; and

2. Where biological evolution is taught, the curriculum should help students to understand why this subject generates so much continuing controversy, and should prepare the students to be informed participants in public discussions regarding the subject.

Source: Speech in "A Senator Speaks Out," pp.101-2, June 13, 2001

Gingrich on Religion in Schools

Voluntary school prayer creates bond between you and Creator

There's a reason why voluntary school prayer mattered, and the reason goes far from the concept of being endowed by our Creator and getting authority from a Supreme Being.

I had a very bright student in the class who said, "Do you really think voluntary school prayer matters that much? Why does it matter? You really think 30 seconds matter?" And I suddenly realized the reason it matters is it establishes at the beginning of the day the concept of a hierarchy. That the teacher is an intermediary between the Creator who is endowing is with our unalienable rights and us.

If there is a Creator and your rights are endowed by the Creator, then there is a direct bond between you and the Creator. Now this is not a violation of church and state. They're not

Source: Newt!, by Dick Williams, pp.172-3, June 1, 1995

Santorum on Church-State Separation

Church-state "neutrality" is not in US Constitution

In 1947 the Supreme Court's majority declared that the "wall between Church and State must be kept high and impregnable." In the Court's eyes, the Constitution's position on religion is one of a "strict and lofty neutrality."

In most cases since then, the question before the Court concerned either prayer in public schools, or public assistance for sectarian (usually Catholic) schools. Just last year, the Supreme Court dodged on a technicality a case that would have removed "under God" from the Pledge of Allegiance: ruling "under God" unconstitutional would have been deeply unpopular, but by the Court's own logic, there is no way to escape the conclusion it must go. The overarching impulse of the Court's position has been to drive religion from the public square, in the name of the constitutional principle "neutrality"—both among religions and between religion and irreligion.

Of course, the term "neutrality" does not appear in the US Constitution. This doctrine is a pure invention of the Court.

Source: It Takes a Family, by Rick Santorum, pp.230-1, April 30, 2006

Gingrich on Church-State Separation

Declaration assumes God created man

One of the Declaration's most famous passages proclaims, "All men are created equal, that they are endowed by their Creator with certain unalienable Rights...." This assertion makes some key assumptions about the relationship between man and God: It assumes that God created man. It assumes that man must obey an order of justice that God has instituted. That order of justice requires all men and women to honor each other's natural rights, because these rights are an unalienable endowment from the Almighty. When someone violates another's rights, he is not merely breaking the law, he is violating God's grant of protection.

Source: A Nation Like No Other, by Newt Gingrich, p. 21, June 13, 2011

Constitution says freedom *of* religion, not *from* religion

The Bill of Rights' Amendment I begins: "Congress shall make no law respecting an establishment of religion, or prohibiting the free exercise thereof."

The language clearly prohibits the establishment of an official national religion, while at the same time protecting the observance of religion in both private and public spaces. In fact, two of the principal authors of the First Amendment, Thomas Jefferson and James Madison, both attended church services in the Capitol building. Therefore, these Founding Fathers clearly saw no conflict in opposing the establishment of an official religion while protecting the freedom of religious expression in the public square.

Source: Rediscovering God in America, by Newt Gingrich, pp. 31-2,
Dec 31, 2006

Santorum on American Faith

Govern via both faith & reason

Q: I'm wondering what your definition of the separation of church and state is?

PAWLENTY: Well, the protections between the separation of church and state were designed to protect people of faith from government, not government from people of faith.

Q: How will that affect your decision-making?

SANTORUM: I'm someone who believes that you approach issues using faith and reason. And if your faith is pure and your reason is right, they'll end up in the same place. I think the key to the success of this country, how we all live together, is because we are a very diverse country. We allow everybody, people of faith and no faith, to come in and make their claims in the public square, to be heard, have those arguments, and not to say because you're no a person of faith, you need to stay out, because you have strong faith convictions, your opinion is invalid. Just the opposite—we get along because we know that we—all of our ideas are allowed in and tolerated. That's what makes America work.

Source: GOP primary debate in Manchester NH, June 13, 2011

Gingrich on American Faith

Five habits of liberty sustain American Exceptionalism

Looking through 400 years of American history, we find five habits of liberty that have been crucial to sustaining American Exceptionalism.

They are: faith and family, work, civil society, rule of law, and safety and peace.

Tempering man's worst impulses, these distinctly American habits are vital to cultivating an engaged, informed citizenry, which is needed to sustain a free republic and secure the unalienable rights asserted in the Declaration of Independence. The emphasis on these habits set America apart from its European counterparts, where monarchs were intent on cultivating passive, obedient subjects unlikely to change their ruler's claim to power.

Source: A Nation Like No Other, by Newt Gingrich, p. 42, June 13, 2011

Santorum on the Tea Party

Tea Party is now the backbone of the conservative movement

Q: What role do you think the Tea Party will play in the 2012 elections?

A: Hopefully as great as they did on the last election. Defending the constitution and limited govt. Thank you!! The Tea Party is now the backbone of the conservative movement. It will help elect a principled conservative leader for 2012.

Source: Republican primary debate on Twitter.com, July 21, 2011

Tea Party should support ideas, not candidates

Q: You said that you were "the Tea Party before there was a Tea Party."

SANTORUM: I didn't say that, the Washington Post said it. I simply commented on what they said. I don't take the claim, the Tea Party organization is flat and it should stay that way. It should support ideas, not candidates. And people who stand up and say they lead it, well, I think most of the Tea Party people think their leadership is among the people not anybody is a member of congress or anywhere else.

Source: Iowa Straw Poll 2011 GOP debate in Ames Iowa, Aug. 11, 2011

Gingrich on the Tea Party

Tea Party prevents mistake of electing conservative Democrats

Q: What role do you think the Tea Party will play in the 2012 elections?

A: Tea Party will help prevent Republicans from making same mistakes of 2004 and 2006 & help elect conservative democrats. The most important role for the Tea Party is not in elections, but in developing local solutions as we move power out of Washington. Permanently ending the age of big government will be hard work and require a team effort between federal, state & local government.

Source: 2011 Republican primary debate on Twitter.com, July 21, 2011

Santorum on Conservative Values

I'm a conservative but not a libertarian; some government OK

Q: Congressman Paul, you've got a new ad up in which you call Santorum a corrupt corporate lobbyist, a Washington insider with a record of betrayal. Are you willing to stand by those charges?

RON PAUL: In a survey, he came out as one of the top corrupt individuals because he took so much money from the lobbyists. But what really counts is his record: he's a big government, big spending individual.

SANTORUM: The group that called me corrupt was a group called CREW. If you haven't been sued by CREW, you're not a conservative. It's a ridiculous charge. I'm a conservative. I'm not a libertarian. I believe in some government. I do believe that as a senator from Pennsylvania that I had a responsibility to go out there and represent the interests of my state. I am not a libertarian, Ron—you vote against everything. I don't vote against everything. I do vote for some spending. I do think government has a role to play.

Source: WMUR GOP New Hampshire debate, Jan. 7, 2012

Gingrich on Conservative Values

Liberals exploit weakness; conservatives offer strength

We must expect liberals to continue to fight us, and where they do so honestly, to respect them for it while continuing to work for our success. But it is well to remember that temptation is something ever lurking, waiting to exploit human weakness, especially in difficult times. What we have to offer people instead is strength and adventure, the experience of a new level of life-enhancing energy and love of a great country. We have no reason to become distressed—as many members of the House did and as I at some point also did. What we are embarked on is what they call steady work, more than enough for a lifetime.

Source: Lessons Learned the Hard Way, by Newt Gingrich, pp. 82-3,
Jul 2, 1998

Red-blue split is 85% Americans and 15% fringe

The media tell us America is a nation divided between conservative red states and liberal blue states. They tell us that red and blue are equally divided—which is why elections are so close, and why Congress seems gridlocked.

But that's simply not true. The reality is the American people are united on almost every important issue facing our country. The real division is between red-white-blue America (about 85% of the country) and a fringe on the left (about 15% of the country). Not only have the media perpetuated the myth that the country is equally divided, but the elites on the left fringe have also insisted that their positions hold moral superiority. Neither is true.

Source: Real Change, by Newt Gingrich, p. 3, Dec. 18, 2007

Santorum vs. Gingrich on International Issues

International issues focus on foreign relations and anything involving foreign nations, including the following topics:

- *Energy and Oil:* including global warming, domestic drilling and alternative energy sources. Sen. Santorum and Rep. Gingrich agree on increasing domestic oil and gas production.

- *Free Trade:* including NAFTA (the North American Free trade Agreement) and other bilateral agreements, plus opinions on the trade organizations like the WTO (World Trade Organization). Both candidates focus on China with little comment about other free trade.

- *Immigration:* including border security; the border fence; and dealing with the current 12 million illegal immigrants in the US. Gingrich focuses on enforcement and regrets having supported Reagan's amnesty; Santorum takes a harder line than Gingrich.

- *Foreign Policy:* Both candidates focus on military solutions rather than diplomatic solutions, in Iran, in Pakistan, and in the Arab world. Gingrich worked with Pres. Bill Clinton on diplomatic aid in the 1990s; Santorum fought against Clinton at the same time.

- *Homeland Security:* this category concerns defense policy, not war policy. This category includes defense spending issues; and defense strategy goals. Both Santorum and Gingrich want dramatic increases in all aspects of defense spending.

- *War and Peace:* including the current ongoing wars in Iraq and Afghanistan. The two candidates agree on staying in Afghanistan, and both would have preferred a longer stay in Iraq. Both agree on a military solution to Iranian nuclear development.

Rick Santorum
on International Issues

Santorum on Global Warming : 114
    Out of office, I stayed in the fray to defeat cap-and-trade

Santorum on Oil Drilling:...116
    Sagging economy caused by stop sign on oil drilling

Santorum on China Trade: 118
    I'm for making US more competitive than China

Santorum on Border Security: 120
    Finish the border fence; make English the official language

Santorum on Guest Workers: 122
    No tricks like 1986; secure the border first

Santorum on Pakistani Nukes: 124
    Deal with Musharraf in Pakistan in advance of trouble

Santorum on Israel/Palestine: 126
    West Bank residents are Israelis; there are no Palestinians

Santorum on Iranian Sanctions: 128
    Iran's theocracy encourages use of nuclear weapons

Santorum on Foreign Aid: 130
    YES on capping foreign aid at only $12.7 billion

Santorum on the Patriot Act: 132
    War against Islamic fascism will be won or lost in America

Santorum on Defense spending: 134
    Don't cut one penny out of defense spending

Santorum on Sources of Terrorism: 136
    Jihadists want to kill us for what we are

Santorum on Unconventional Weapons: 138
    Terrorism is an asymmetric threat; we need worldwide bases

Santorum on Iraq War: 140
    We need 20,000 troops to stay in Iraq to achieve victory

Santorum on Afghanistan War: 142
    Stay in Afghanistan until security of our country is secure

Newt Gingrich
on International Issues

Gingrich on Global Warming : 115
    Kyoto treaty is bad for the environment and bad for America
Gingrich on Oil Drilling: 117
    2008 book: Drill Here, Drill Now, Pay Less
Gingrich on China Trade: 119
    Protectionism helps China & India challenge US supremacy
Gingrich on Border Security: 121
    Review all illegal aliens & if you have no ties, go home
Gingrich on Guest Workers: 123
    I voted for Reagan's legal guest worker program
Gingrich on Pakistani Nukes: 125
    Contain nuclear threats: China, Russia, Pakistan, North Korea
Gingrich on Israel/Palestine: 127
    Tell the truth: Palestinians are an "invented people"
Gingrich on Iranian Sanctions: 129
    Sabotage Iran's oil refinery
Gingrich on Foreign Aid: 131
    1993: $1.6B Russia aid package was "great defining moment"
Gingrich on the Patriot Act: 133
    Defend America & allies with information policies
Gingrich on Defense spending: 135
    Defense as percentage of GDP is lowest since WWII
Gingrich on Sources of Terrorism: 137
    The "Irreconcilable Wing of Islam" threatens our way of life
Gingrich on Unconventional Weapons: 139
    Biological threat bigger than nuclear threat
Gingrich on Iraq War: 141
    Goal was to liberate Iraq from Saddam, not to occupy
Gingrich on Afghanistan War: 143
    We have mismanaged region-wide crisis in Middle East

Santorum on Global Warming

Out of office, I stayed in the fray to defeat cap-and-trade

Rep. RON PAUL: Where did Santorum make his living after [leaving the Senate]? He became a high-powered lobbyist in Washington, D.C. And he has done quite well.

SANTORUM: I was known in Washington, D.C., as a "cause guy." I care deeply about this country and about the causes that I think are at the core of this country. When I left the US Senate, I got involved in causes that I believe in. I was asked by a health care company to be on their board of directors. Now, I don't know whether you think board of directors are lobbyists. They're not. I also worked for a coal company. When I left the Senate, one of the big issues on the table was cap-and-trade, global warming, and I wanted to stay involved in the fray. So I contacted a local coal company from my area, and I said, look, I want to join you in that fight. I want to work together with you. I want to help you in any way I can to make sure we defeat cap-and-trade. And so I engaged in that battle. And I'm very proud to have engaged in that battle.

Source: WMUR 2012 GOP New Hampshire debate, Jan. 7, 2012

NOTE: "Cap-and-Trade" refers to a carbon dioxide (CO_2) emissions policy where the amount of CO_2 is "capped" at a government-specified emission amount, and then the right to emit CO_2 is "traded" via emission permits. A similar program was used successfully to battle acid rain via sulfur dioxide emission permits trading on the Chicago Mercantile Exchange.

Gingrich on Global Warming

Kyoto treaty is bad for the environment and bad for America

Kyoto is a bad treaty. It is bad for the environment and it is bad for America. It sets standards that will require massive investments by the US but virtually no investments by other countries. The Senate was right when it voted unanimously against the treaty. We should insist on revisiting the entire Kyoto process and resolutely reject efforts to force us into an anti-American, environmentally failed treaty.

The US should support substantial research into climate science, managing the response to climate change, & in developing new non-carbon energy systems. It is astounding to watch people blithely propose trillions of dollars in spending on a topic on which we have failed to spend modest amounts to better understand.

It is astounding to have people focus myopically on carbon as the sole source of climate change. The world's climate has changed in the past with sudden speed and dramatic impact. Global warming may happen. On the other hand it is possible Europe will experience another ice age.

Source: Gingrich Communications website, www.newt.org, Dec. 1, 2006

NOTE: "Kyoto" refers to a Climate Change Treaty which sets carbon dioxide reduction targets for the US and other developed countries. Completed in 1998, the US has not yet signed. This is politically controversial because it would require the US to cut CO_2 emissions, which is potentially costly.

Santorum on Oil Drilling

Sagging economy caused by stop sign on oil drilling

Q: Gov. Pawlenty laid out an economic plan in which he said you could grow the economy 5% a year. Is that too optimistic?

SANTORUM: I think we need a president who's optimistic, who has a pro-growth agenda. I'm not going to comment on 5% or 4%. What we need is an economy that's unshackled. And what's happened in this administration is that they have passed oppressive regulation—Obamacare being first and foremost. Throw on top of that what this president's done on energy. The reason we're seeing this second dip is because of energy prices, and this president has put a stop sign again—against oil drilling, against any kind of exploration offshore or in Alaska, and that is depressing. We need to drill. We need to create energy jobs, just like we're doing in Pennsylvania, where we're drilling 3,000 wells this year for gas, and natural gas prices are down as a result.

Source: GOP primary debate in Manchester NH, June 13, 2011

No federal energy help needed; we did it on Marcellus Shale

Q: North Dakota has the largest oil discovery in a generation. Would you favor incentives to support this boom?

A: No, because we have done it in Pennsylvania, the Marcellus Shale. It took a while for us to ramp up, but we're drilling 3,000 wells. The price of natural gas, because of Marcellus Shale, has gone from $12 to $3.65. And we let the marketplace work. So, no, we didn't have the federal government come in and bail us out.

Source: CNBC GOP Primary debate in Rochester MI, Nov. 9, 2011

Gingrich on Oil Drilling

2008 book: Drill Here, Drill Now, Pay Less

In 2008, American Solutions launched an online petition drive to demand Congress lift the 25-year-old moratorium on new offshore drilling. We collected 1.5 million signatures. Our effort sparked a nationwide grassroots rebellion that resulted in Congress allowing the moratorium to expire.

I wrote a book in fall 2008 called "Drill Here, Drill Now, Pay Less," describing America's vast energy potential and explain how misguided government policies have prevented us from becoming an energy powerhouse.

Source: Real Change, by Newt Gingrich, pp.205-6, Dec. 18, 2007

2008 petition drive: Drill here, Drill now, Pay less

In 2008 when gasoline was at $4 a gallon, American Solutions launched a petition drive: Drill here, Drill now, Pay less.

The Left couldn't survive in a world where we had the courage to say, "Why don't we find American oil and why don't we find American gas, and why don't we have the next building boom in the United States, not in Dubai. And why don't we make sure that the terrorists run out of money?" And that ought to be our approach to this, so let's do it now.

First of all: Reopen off of Louisiana. The people of Louisiana want it to happen. So let's reopen the areas off only those states that want to reopen them. Let's let them do it now.

Source: Speech at Conservative Political Action Conference, Feb. 11, 2011

Santorum on China Trade

I'm for making US more competitive than China

ROMNEY [on videotape]: I will label China as it is, a currency manipulator. If they cheat, there is a price to pay. I certainly don't want a trade war with anybody, and we're not going to have a trade war, but we can't have a trade surrender either.

SANTORUM: You know, I don't want to go to a trade war. I want to beat China. I want to go war with China and make America the most attractive place in the world to do business, and we need to do that with the agenda that I've outlined.

Source: GOP debate at Dartmouth College, NH, Oct. 11, 2011

Gingrich on China Trade

Protectionism helps China & India
challenge US supremacy

In the US, there exists a coalition of union leaders who prefer protection over competition. This liberal coalition complains about companies' outsourcing jobs while insisting on corporate taxes that encourage companies to go overseas. They prefer that government impose on business obsolete, absurd work rules, even though these raise costs, lower productivity, and make America less competitive in the world market.

The challenge to American economic supremacy from 1.3 billion Chinese and more than 1.1 billion Indians is vastly greater than anything we have previously seen. India's embrace of capitalism and China's bizarre combination of Marxist-Leninist government and free market initiatives will create a future where one-fourth of the world's markets will be controlled by these countries. Those who advocate economic isolationism and protectionism are advocating a policy that could help China and India surpass the US in economic power in our children's or grandchildren's lifetime.

Source: Gingrich Communications website, www.newt.org, Dec. 1, 2006

Santorum on Border Security

Finish the border fence;
make English the official language

Q: What would you do about illegal immigrants?

SANTORUM: I'm the son of an Italian immigrant. I believe in immigration, as an important part of the lifeblood of this country. But what we have is a problem of an unsecure border. Unlike Gov. Perry, I believe we need to build more fence. I believe that we need to secure the border using technology and more personnel. And until we build that border, we should neither have storm troopers come in and throw people out of the country nor should we provide amnesty.

PERRY: The idea that you're going to build a wall from Brownsville to El Paso and go left for another 800 miles to Tijuana is just not reality.

SANTORUM: What Gov. Perry's done is he provided in-state tuition for illegal immigrants. Maybe that was an attempt to attract the illegal vote—I mean, the Latino voters. But you attract Latino voters by talking about the importance of immigration. You talk about the importance of having English as the official language of this country.

Source: Tea Party debate in Tampa FL, Sept. 12, 2011

Gingrich on Border Security

Use National Guard on US-Mexican border

Q: If two adults came into this country illegally, and they have a child, should that child be considered a citizen of the US?

CAIN: I don't believe so. But let's look at solving the real problem, OK? #1, get serious about securing our borders. #2, enforce the laws that are already there. #3, promote a path to citizenship by cleaning up the bureaucracy.

GINGRICH: Herman Cain's essentially right, you break it down. First of all, you control the border. We can ask the National Guard to go to Iraq. Somehow we would have done more for American security if we had had the National Guard on the border.

Source: GOP primary debate in Manchester NH, June 13, 2011

Review all illegal aliens & if you have no ties, go home

Q: Back in the '80s, you voted for legislation that had a pathway to citizenship for illegal immigrants.

GINGRICH: I did vote for the Simpson-Mazzoli Act. I believe ultimately you have to find some system that reviews the people who are here. If you've come here recently, you have no ties to this country, you ought to go home. If you've been here 25 years and you got three kids and two grandkids, you've been paying taxes and obeying the law, you belong to a local church, I don't think we're going to separate you from your family, and kick you out.

Source: CNN National Security GOP primary debate, Nov. 22, 2011

Santorum on Guest Workers

No tricks like 1986; secure the border first

Q: There are 11 million illegals that are here. What do you do with them if you are able to secure the border?

A: We can have the discussion [afterwards, based on] how long they've been here, whether they had other types of records. But to have that discussion right now and pull the same trick that was pulled in 1986—we said, well, we'll promise to do this if you do that—no more. We are going to secure the border first, and that's the most important, then we'll have the discussion afterwards.

Source: GOP debate in Simi Valley CA at the Reagan Library, Sept. 7, 2011

Gingrich on Guest Workers

I voted for Reagan's legal guest worker program

Q: Your current perception on immigration reform is a little different on your initial positions under Reagan?

GINGRICH: I think we have to find a way to get to a country in which everybody who's here is here legally. But you referenced President Reagan. In 1986, I voted for the Simpson-Mazzoli Act, which in fact did grant some amnesty in return for promises. President Reagan wrote in his diary that year that he signed the act because we were going to control the border and we were going to have an employer program where it was a legal guest worker program. That's in his diary. I'm with President Reagan. We ought to control the border, we ought to have a legal guest worker program. We ought to outsource it, frankly, to American Express, Visa, and MasterCard, so there's no counterfeiting, which there will be with the federal government. We should be very tough on employers once you have that legal program.

Source: 2011 GOP debate in Simi Valley CA at the Reagan Library,
Sep 7, 2011

NOTE: The "Simpson-Mazzoli Act" refers to the Immigration Reform and Control Act of 1986, was the immigration reform supported by President Reagan. Its opponents claimed that it granted amnesty in exchange for tightening immigration law, but that the tightening never occurred while the amnesty did.

Santorum on Pakistani Nukes

Deal with Musharraf in Pakistan in advance of trouble

Q: Would Iran get Pakistani nukes in a coup?

SANTORUM: We should be establishing relationships in Pakistan with allies of ours, folks like President Musharraf. So if in fact something like [a coup] would occur, we could work in concert to make sure that that coup could be overturned and make sure those nuclear weapon do not fall in those hands. But working with allies at that point is the last thing we want to do. We want to work in that country to make sure the problem is defused.

Source: GOP Google debate in Orlando FL, Sept. 22, 2011

NOTE: Pakistan and their nemesis India both successfully tested nuclear weapons in 1998. Neither country signed the Nuclear Test Ban Treaty, and hence their nuclear test were not subject to international criticism. Iran, in contrast, signed the Nuclear Test Ban Treaty in 1996 and hence is subject to international criticism for developing nuclear weapons. North Korea never signed the treaty, but was criticized internationally anyway for its first nuclear test in 2006. Pakistan and India have about 100 nuclear warheads each, compared to 8,500 possessed by the United States; 11,000 possessed by Russia; and fewer than 10 possessed by North Korea.

Gingrich on Pakistani Nukes

Contain nuclear threats:
China, Russia, Pakistan, North Korea

Every day, terrorists try to acquire weapons of mass destruction & weapons of mass murder. Iran & North Korea continue to develop their nuclear and other weapons programs. There is constant danger of a coup by radical Islamists in nuclear-armed Pakistan.

And the greatest danger for us in meeting this threat is the weakness of our intelligence services. We do not have any significant intelligence on the enemy's plans, networks, & troop strength.

Second, we must contain powers that could threaten us, including China, Russia, North Korea, Iran, & Pakistan—all of which have weapons of mass destruction.

The greatest threat of rogue dictatorships, like Iran or North Korea, is that they will sell weapons of mass destruction. While North Korea—with nuclear, chemical, & biological weapons—is a big threat to South Korea & Japan, it is a very distant threat to the US. But an Iran or a North Korea willing to sell nuclear and biological weapons to terrorists is very dangerous to America.

Source: Gingrich Communications website, www.newt.org, "Issues",
Sept. 1, 2007

Santorum on Israel/Palestine

West Bank residents are Israelis; there are no Palestinians

Quote: "All the people who live in the West Bank are Israelis, they're not Palestinians. There is no 'Palestinian.' This is Israeli land." (Campaign stop in Iowa, Nov. 18, 2011)

Reaction: "His comments represent an even more conservative position than that taken by the Israeli government," says The Washington Post. Israel's anti-Palestinian position itself isn't "accepted by much of the world, but it seems that a potential US president should accept the definitions used by the Israeli government."

Source: Santorum's "9 most controversial statements" in The Week
Jan 5, 2012

NOTE: Britain controlled both Israel and Palestine as a colony known as "The British Mandate in Palestine" prior to 1948. On May 14, 1948, the United Nations (with US support, but without Arab support) declared the region partitioned into two states, Israel and Palestine. Neighboring Arab countries immediately invaded; Israel survived the ensuing war but Palestine did not. Egypt, Syria, and Jordan occupied areas which the UN had declared as parts of Palestine. Israel also occupied some of those areas in 1948, and all of those areas in 1967, but Israel agrees that eventually there should be two states. Gingrich and Santorum claim that "Palestine" does not exist; they mean that it was only an independent legal nation for a very brief period in 1948. But the "Palestinian" identity did exist prior to 1948, and has become the self-identification of Arabs living within the current Israeli borders.

Gingrich on Israel/Palestine

Tell the truth: Palestinians are an "invented people"

Q: You caused a stir in the Middle East by calling the Palestinians "an invented people." The chief Palestinian negotiator said, "These statements of Gingrich will be the ammunition of the bin Ladens and the extremists for a long, long time."

GINGRICH: How would he know the difference? Look, is what I said factually correct? Yes. Is it historically true? Yes. Are we in a situation where every day, rockets are fired into Israel while the US tries to pressure the Israelis into a peace process? A Palestinian Authority ambassador said, "There is no difference between Fatah and Hamas. We both agree Israel has no right to exist." Somebody ought to have the courage to tell the truth: These people are terrorists. They teach terrorism in their schools. They have textbooks that say, "If there are 13 Jews and nine Jews are killed, how many Jews are left?" We pay for those textbooks through our aid money. It's time for somebody to have the guts to stand up and say, "Enough lying about the Middle East."

Source: Yahoo's "Your Voice Your Vote" debate in Iowa, Dec. 10, 2011

Santorum on Iranian Sanctions

Iran's theocracy encourages use of nuclear weapons

Q: Why is it that we cannot live with a nuclear Iran?

SANTORUM: They're a theocracy. They're a theocracy that has deeply embedded beliefs that the afterlife is better than this life. President Ahmadinejad has repeatedly said the principal virtue of the Islamic Republic of Iran is martyrdom. So when your principal virtue is to die for Allah, then it's not a deterrent to have a nuclear threat if they would use a nuclear weapon. It is, in fact, an encouragement for them to use their nuclear weapon, and that's why there's a difference between the Soviet Union and China and others and Iran.

Source: Meet the Press GOP New Hampshire debate, Jan. 8, 2012

Work with Israel to take out Iranian nukes by force

GINGRICH: [To avoid Iran gaining a nuclear weapon, we need] coordination with the Israelis, in a way which allows them to maximize their impact in Iran. And if despite those things, the dictatorship persists, you have to take whatever steps are necessary to break its capacity to have a nuclear weapon.

SANTORUM: I disagree with Newt: more sanctions and providing more support for the pro-democracy movement isn't going to be enough. We should be working with Israel right now to do what they did in Syria, what they did in Iraq, which is take out that nuclear capability before the next explosion we hear in Iran is a nuclear one and then the world changes.

Source: 2011 debate in South Carolina on Foreign Policy, Nov. 12, 2011

Gingrich on Iranian Sanctions

Sabotage Iran's oil refinery

Gov. PERRY: [to Gingrich]: We need to sanction the Iranian Central Bank. That will shut down that economy.

GINGRICH: We ought to have a massive all-sources energy program, designed to literally replace the Iranian oil. Now that's how we won World War II. We all get sucked into these tactical discussions. We need a strategy of defeating and replacing the current Iranian regime with minimum use of force. But if we were serious, we could break the Iranian regime, I think, within a year, starting candidly with cutting off the gasoline supply to Iran, and then, frankly, sabotaging the only refinery they have.

Q: But sanctions on the Iranian Central Bank now, is that a good idea or a bad idea?

GINGRICH: I think it's a good idea if you're serious about stopping them. I think replacing the regime before they get a nuclear weapon without a war beats replacing the regime with war, which beats allowing them to have a nuclear weapon. Those are your three choices.

Source: 2011 CNN National Security GOP primary debate Nov. 22, 2011

Santorum on Foreign Aid

Voted YES on capping foreign aid at only $12.7 billion

Vote on adoption of the 2000 Foreign Operations Appropriations Bill providing $12.7 billion for foreign aid programs in 2000. Status: Agreed to 51-49.

Oct. 18 1999 Veto message by President: The overall funding provided by H.R. 2606 is inadequate. It is about half the amount available in real terms to President Reagan in 1985, and it is 14% below the level that I requested. By denying America a decent investment in diplomacy, this bill suggests we should meet threats to our security with our military might alone. That is a dangerous proposition. For if we underfund our diplomacy, we will end up overusing our military.

Source: H.R. 2606 Conference Report; vote number 312 on Oct. 6, 1999

NOTE: The total amount of foreign aid in recent years is listed below. The foreign aid allocation, while controversial, is not economically large: it represents 1.5% of federal expenditures ($47.6 billion out of $1.3 trillion in 2009). Total foreign aid is broken down into military and non-military components.

Billions / year	Economic Assistance	Military Assistance
2000	$13.2	$4.9
2001	$12.9	$3.9
2002	$15.2	$4.8
2003	$19.1	$6.7
2004	$27.4	$6.1
2005	$29.7	$7.4
2006	$27.1	$12.3
2007	$27.7	$13.2
2008	$33.0	$15.9
2009	$33.9	$13.7

Gingrich on Foreign Aid

1993: $1.6B Russia aid package was "great defining moment"

In March 1993, I got an assistance program I could support: $1.6 billion in direct aid to help Russia stabilize.

Although a public poll said that 75% of the American people were opposed to giving Russia more money, and we were already in a hard fight for the economic plan, I felt we had no choice but to press ahead. American had spent trillions of dollars in defense to win the Cold War; we couldn't risk reversal over less than $2 billion and a bad poll. To the surprise of my staff, the congressional leaders, including the Republicans, agreed with me. At a meeting I convened to push the plan, Senator Joe Biden, the chairman of the Foreign Relations Committee, strongly endorsed the aid package.

Newt Gingrich was passionately in favor of helping Russia, saying it was a "great defining moment" for American and we had to do the right thing. Newt was trying to "out-Russia" me, which I was only too happy to have him do.

Source: My Life, by Bill Clinton, p.506-507, June 21, 2004

Santorum on the Patriot Act

War against Islamic fascism
will be won or lost in America

CASEY: Rick, you just talked about Iran, calling it "Islamic fascism"[instead of terrorism]. What we need, Rick, is not a change in the terminology, we need to change the tactics. We should be finding and killing Osama bin Laden, then we can hold a seminar on whether he's a dead terrorist or a dead fascist.

SANTORUM: My opponent has no plan. All you suggested with your plan is more Special Forces. Do you support more intelligence gathering?

CASEY: Absolutely.

SANTORUM: The Democratic Party has gone out and said that you have serious questions about our intelligence surveillance programs.

CASEY: You're debating me, not the Party. We should keep the programs and keep the wiretaps.

SANTORUM: I think you just fundamentally misunderstand the problem. You're saying that somehow or another the terminology doesn't matter. You believe that we're going to win or lose this war on the battlefield in Iraq and Afghanistan. I don't. I think we'll win or lose this war right here in America.

Source: Meet the Press: PA 2006 Senate Debate, Tim Russert moderator,
Sep 3, 2006

Gingrich on the Patriot Act

Defend America & allies with information policies

We must implement policies that will ensure America's leadership, safety, and prosperity. To achieve this future we will defend America and our allies from those who would destroy us. To achieve security, we will develop the intelligence, diplomatic, information, defense, and homeland security systems and resources for success.

Source: Gingrich Communications website, www.newt.org, Dec. 1, 2006

All of us will be in danger for the rest of our lives

I think looking at [terrorism] carefully [we should] extend [the PATRIOT Act] and build an honest understanding that all of us will be in danger for the rest of our lives. This is not going to end in the short run. And we need to be prepared to protect ourselves from those who, if they could, would not just kill us individually, but would take out entire cities.

Source: 2011 CNN National Security GOP primary debate, Nov. 22, 2011

Santorum on Defense Spending

Don't cut one penny out of defense spending

Q: [to Paul]: You proposed a 15% cut to the Defense Department. Can you guarantee national security will not be hurt by that?

Rep. RON PAUL: I think it would be enhanced. I don't want to cut any defense. There's a lot of money spent in the military budget that doesn't do any good for our defense.

SANTORUM: I would absolutely not cut one penny out of military spending. The only thing the federal government can do that no other level of government can do is protect us. It is the first duty of the president. And we should have all the resources in place to make sure that we can defend our borders, that we can make sure that when we engage in foreign countries, we do so to succeed. That has been the problem in this administration. We've had political objectives instead of objectives for success. And that's why we haven't succeeded.

PAUL: Well, I think we're on economic suicide if we're not even willing to look at some of these overseas expenditures, 900 bases, 150 different countries. We have enough weapons to blow up the world about 20-25 times. We have more weapons than all the other countries put together essentially. And we want to spend more and more, and you can't cut a penny?

Source: GOP primary debate in Las Vegas, Oct. 18, 2011

Gingrich on Defense Spending

Defense as percentage of GDP is lowest since WWII

Q: How do you weigh the cost of fighting the war on terror against the exploding debt crisis?

GINGRICH: The exploding debt crisis is because of exploding politician spending in Washington, not because of national security.

SANTORUM: The first priority of the federal government is to keep America safe. I would not cut defense—freeze it; cut waste; and then plow savings back into Defense.

Gov. GARY JOHNSON: The debt is the greatest threat to national security we face today. Besides, we do not need 60,000 to 100,000 troops in Afghanistan and Iraq to protect ourselves. Nor do we need nation-building.

GINGRICH: We spend less on defense today as percentage of GDP than at any time since Pearl Harbor.

SANTORUM: The first priority of the federal government is to keep America safe. I would not cut defense—freeze it; cut waste; and then plow savings back into Defense.

GINGRICH: Controlling the border and defending America are job #1 under the Constitution.

Source: Republican primary debate on Twitter.com, July 21, 2011

Santorum on Sources of Terrorism

Jihadists want to kill us for what we are

Rep. RON PAUL: [to Santorum]: We're under great threat, because we occupy so many countries. We're in 130 countries. We're there occupying their land. And if we think that we can do that and not have retaliation, we're kidding ourselves.

SANTORUM: On your Web site on 9/11, you had a blog post that basically blamed the United States for 9/11. On your Web site, yesterday, you said that it was our actions that brought about the actions of 9/11. Now, that is irresponsible. Someone who is running for the president of the United States in the Republican Party should not be parroting what Osama bin Laden said on 9/11. We are not being attacked and we were not attacked because of our actions. We were attacked because we have a civilization that is antithetical to the civilization of the jihadists. And they want to kill us because of who we are and what we stand for. And we stand for American exceptionalism, we stand for freedom and opportunity for everybody around the world, and I am not ashamed to do that.

Source: Tea Party debate in Tampa FL, Sept. 12, 2011

Confront virulent threat of radical Islam

Gov. JON HUNTSMAN: So how long do you want to wait, Rick? How long do you want to wait to get out of Afghanistan?

SANTORUM: Until the security of our country is ensured. That's what the job of the commander-in-chief is. And you make that decision based on an analysis of understanding how virulent the threat of radical Islam is.

Source: WMUR GOP New Hampshire debate, Jan. 7, 2012

Gingrich on Sources of Terrorism

The "Irreconcilable Wing of Islam" threatens our way of life

Beyond the Petraeus Report, we need a report on the larger war with the Irreconcilable Wing of Islam. This enemy is irreconcilable with the modern civilized world because its values would block any woman from being in this room, having a job, voting, being education. It is irreconcilable because it cannot tolerate other religions or other lifestyles. It represents what some have called an Islamofascist approach to imposing its views on others and as such it is a moral threat to our way of life, to freedom, and to the rule of law.

The Irreconcilable Wing of Islam has emerged as an extremist movement against not only non-Muslims but also against moderate Muslims who wish both to preserve their faith and to be a part of the modern world.

Source: Real Change, by Newt Gingrich, p.292, Dec. 18, 2007

Santorum on Unconventional Weapons

Terrorism is an asymmetric threat; we need worldwide bases

Q: We're in debt up to our eyeballs. We have nation building going on around the world. We're the world's police force. World War II is over. The Korean War is over. But we still have military bases all over Europe, all over Asia. Are you willing to shut down the bases that aren't vital to our national security, and take that money to pay off our national debt?

SANTORUM: We have actually closed down a lot of bases overseas. Look, what we're dealing with is a failure of leadership on this administration's part to actually put together a strategy where we can confront our enemies. And our enemies are asymmetric threats: terrorism. That means that they are not just positioned in the Middle East, but around the world. That means we have to have the ability to confront those threats from around the world, which means we need basing around the world. We do need that basing. We do need to be able to be nimble and to be able to attack where we're attacked because it's not just a threat.

Source: GOP primary debate in Manchester NH, June 13, 2011

Gingrich on Unconventional Weapons

Biological threat bigger than nuclear threat

Biological warfare is the largest threat to the human race, a substantially bigger threat than nuclear war. If the US is hit with an engineered biological agent for which no vaccines are available, we are in for problems of colossal proportions.

Biological threats for which we have no rapid diagnostic tests & no drug treatments are so great that we should consider the preparation of a biological defensive system the highest priority in the American national security system and the most important job facing the new DHS.

In thinking about weapons of mass destruction, a good rule of thumb is to put 80% of our effort into dealing with biological threats, 19.5% into nuclear threats, and 0.5% into chemical weapons. Six key areas must be addressed:

1. Vision and strategy design

2. Information technology investment

3. Vaccinations and immunization

4. Post-event treatment

5. Civil defense transformation into a comprehensive 21st-century system

6. Biosecurity and education.

Source: Saving Lives and Saving Money, by Newt Gingrich, pp.275-84,
Sep 22, 2003

Santorum on Iraq War

We need 20,000 troops to stay in Iraq to achieve victory

Q: If the security situation were to fall apart in Iraq in 2012 would you support sending US troops back to the region to stabilize the gains made?

SANTORUM: I'm not for taking them out of the region. I believe we need to listen to our generals, and our generals are being very, very clear that we need to continue to stabilize Iraq, the Iraqi government wants and needs our intelligence in particular, needs force protection. We need to have—I'm hearing numbers of 20,000 to 30,000 troops potentially to remain in Iraq, not indefinitely, but to continue to make sure that this is a stable transition. When it comes to this issue, I stand up and say that when we engage in Iraq and Afghanistan, we engage because we want to be successful. We want victory. We want to have accomplished a national security objective for this country to make sure that we are safer. We are not on a political agenda to withdraw troops. So the first thing is to make sure that we secure success.

Source: GOP Google debate in Orlando FL, Sept. 22, 2011

Gingrich on Iraq War

Goal was to liberate Iraq from Saddam, not to occupy

No one in the initial war planning expected the US would try to run Iraq after defeating Saddam. There was a general belief that portions of the Iraqi army could be converted in to a policing force.

It was vital from day one that the US be seen as a liberator and not as an occupier. For some reason the lesson learned in Afghanistan—of liberating and not occupying—did not get across. Like most bureaucracies, this one looked after itself. It created a green zone of protection and comfort to shield the bureaucrats. By creating a green zone, it acknowledged that the entire rest of the country was a red zone, a danger zone. Worst of all, the decision to have an explicitly American administrator of Iraq guaranteed that America's role would change from liberator to occupier.

By Dec. 2003, things were so bad that I went public and declared that we had "gone off a cliff" in the June decisions, and that until they were reversed things were just going to get worse.

Source: Real Change, by Newt Gingrich, pp.110-1, Dec. 18, 2007

Santorum on Afghanistan War

Stay in Afghanistan until security of our country is secure

Q: Would you send troops back into Iraq right now?

SANTORUM: Well, I wouldn't right now, but we need someone who has a strong vision for the region and we have not had that with this president. [Obama] has made mistakes on the ground that have shown the people in that region that we are the weak horse. America is soft and so they can be pushed around. They did it by withdrawing from Iraq, and [the same] if we get out of Afghanistan. Let's just wait and see how things turn out when the United States isn't there and see how consequential our efforts were for the stability of that region.

Gov. JON HUNTSMAN: So how long do you want to wait?

SANTORUM: Until the security of our country is ensured.

Source: WMUR 2012 GOP New Hampshire debate, Jan. 7, 2012

Afghanistan victory means Taliban is neutered, not wiped out

Q: Would you define victory in Afghanistan?

SANTORUM: Victory against the Taliban in Afghanistan is that the Taliban is a neutered force. They are no longer a security threat to the Afghan people or to our country. That would be victory. It doesn't mean wipe them out, we can't wipe them out, but they're no longer a security threat.

Source: 2011 debate in South Carolina on Foreign Policy, Nov. 12, 2011

Gingrich on Afghanistan War

We have mismanaged region-wide crisis in Middle East

Q: When should our 90,000 troops in Afghanistan should be brought home?

GINGRICH: I think we're asking the wrong questions. Afghanistan is a tiny piece of a gigantic mess that is very dangerous. Pakistan is unstable and they probably have between 100 and 200 nuclear weapons. Iran is actively trying to get nuclear weapons. They go out and practice closing the Strait of Hormuz, where one out of every six barrels of oil goes through every day. You have the Muslim Brotherhood winning the elections in Egypt. The truth is, we don't know who's in charge in Libya. You have a region-wide crisis, which we have been mismanaging and underestimating, which is not primarily a military problem. We're not going to go in and solve Pakistan militarily. We're not going to go in and solve all these other things. We need a fundamentally new strategy for the region comparable to what we developed to fight the cold war. And I think it's a very big, hard, long-term problem, but it's not primarily a military problem.

Source: WMUR 2012 GOP New Hampshire debate, Jan. 7, 2012

Book Reviews

OnTheIssues excerpts political books and debates as the primary source of the materials in this book. Following are several book reviews, plus links online to additional books and debates cited in this book.

Book reviews:

A Nation Like No Other, by Speaker Newt Gingrich (2011) ...146

It Takes a Family, by Sen. Rick Santorum (2006)...................148

A Senator Speaks Out, edited by Monument Press (2005) 149

Real Change, by Newt Gingrich (2007) 152

Rediscovering God in America, by Newt Gingrich (2006) 154

Additional book excerpts online:

Saving Lives and Saving Money, by Newt Gingrich (2003)
 www.OnTheIssues.org/Saving_Lives.htm

Lessons Learned the Hard Way, by Newt Gingrich (1998)
 www.OnTheIssues.org/The_Hard_Way.htm

Newt! The 2nd American Revolution, by Dick Williams (1995)
 www.OnTheIssues.org/Newt_Revolution.htm

Book Review:
A Nation Like No Other:
Why American Exceptionalism Matters
by Speaker Newt Gingrich
(June 13, 2011)

The concept of "American Exceptionalism" will permeate the 2011-2012 GOP primary, and likely the 2012 general election as well. Newt Gingrich attempts to out-exception his GOP rivals here, by dedicating an entire book to the concept. We surveyed our non-pundit readers and discovered that the term itself has not yet entered the general voter lexicon—so we will first define it and then analyze its implications here, in anticipation of its usage in upcoming debates.

American exceptionalism means that America has a unique status in the world today, as the sole superpower, and that U.S. policy should work towards recognizing and maintaining that unique status. In contrast to previous nations which ruled the world, America is non-imperialist: previous nations ruled "empires" by occupying territory for the gain of the occupying nation, whereas America establishes bases abroad to enforce the rule of international law and to secure democracy.

Gingrich's definition focuses on the necessary military buildup required to maintain America's unique role (p. 164), as well as on a spiritual basis as its underlying cause (p. 21 & 85). Gingrich previously authored a book, Real Change, expounding upon the need for a larger military; and wrote another book, Rediscovering God in America, outlining the spiritual basis of American society; this book joins those two themes together.

The GOP's interest in American exceptionalism counters Obama's rejection of the concept. When asked in 2009, Obama responded, "Sure, I believe in American exceptionalism in the same way the British believe in British exceptionalism and the Greeks believe in Greek exceptionalism." Republicans generally interpret that as meaning, "No, I don't believe in your version of American exceptionalism at all."

The GOP infer in that disagreement a self-fulfilling prophecy that America is in decline; i.e., that by denying America's role as the sole international superpower, America will eventually doom herself to not being the sole international superpower.

The Left—and Rick Santorum—view American exceptionalism as just another form of imperialism. Does it matter to the people of Saudi Arabia that our bases there "protect" them from enemies in common with their dictator's enemies? Do the people of Cuba feel like the U.S. military base at Guantanamo Bay is not a land grab like any other historical invasion? No, say Chomsky and others, all imperialists justified their invasions as for the good of the world, and probably meant it as much as America does today.

Gingrich chose to publish this book at the start of the primary campaign, hence positioning American Exceptionalism as the theme for his presidential candidacy. Rick Santorum warns the opposite of Gingrich's recommendation of American Exceptionalism: If America unilaterally maintains a large military abroad, America will collapse economically.

We'll see in a few decades whether Gingrich or Rick Santorum were right. But I suspect we'll see in a few months that Gingrich was wrong about making Exceptionalism his campaign theme. Gingrich brilliantly implemented the Contract With America in 1984, with his hand solidly on the pulse of the electorate. But now, not only is Gingrich's hand no longer on the electorate's pulse, but Gingrich seems to not even know where to find their wrist at all. This book just screams "out of touch with the American public."

Book review written July 2011;
full excerpts available online at:
www.ontheissues.org/Nation_No_Other.htm

Book Review: It Takes a Family
Conservatism and the Common Good
by Sen. Rick Santorum (April 30, 2006)

This book is a response to Sen. Hillary Clinton's book *It Takes a Village*. Hillary's book is the liberal perspective on family values; this book is the conservative response. In Sen. Santorum's view, the phrase "It Takes a Village" really means big government (p. 101). Santorum derisively describes the "village elders" who make the decisions in Hillary's "village" as liberals who want control of society. In contrast, conservatives focus on the traditional mother-father-children family unit, explicitly excluding same-sex marriage, of course, and apologetically excluding one-parent families.

Sen. Santorum provides an analysis of "moral capital" as lacking in current society, analogous to "social capital," which means society's institutions. In Santorum's view, de-emphasizing the family has caused the loss of moral capital, and hence decreases the morality of society in general. He also analyzes "intellectual capital" in his extensive education policy sections. Santorum's bigger-picture analysis, beyond family issues, is summarized by: "You can tell whether someone is a conservative or a liberal after only one question: Do you think the Sixties were good for America?" Santorum prefers the family values of the Fifties.

Santorum describes further why he wrote this book (p. 4), in addition to the response to Hillary's book:

"In this book, I hope to show that this all-too-common caricature of conservatives and their social policies by the liberal elite can be attributed to liberals' fundamentally different vision for America—a vision that is completely at odds with that of our nation's founders, and with the views of most Americans today. Liberalism is an ideology; conservatism is common sense."

Sen. Santorum is now running for President, but wasn't when he wrote this book in 2005, At that time, he was running for re-election in the Senate—a race he lost to conservative Democrat Bob Casey.

Santorum has not written a new book yet for the 2012 race, so this book has to serve as his policy outline for the presidential contest

Book review written Aug. 2011;
full excerpts available online at:
www.ontheissues.org/Takes_Family.htm

Book Review: Rick Santorum:

A Senator Speaks Out on Life, Freedom, and Responsibility

Monument Press, ed., (June 8, 2005)

This book is part of the "Modern American Statesmen Series," which re-publishes speeches from the Congressional Record. That means they select speeches which Santorum delivered on the Senate floor. There is no author and no editor; just an introductory note from the publisher (Monument Press) stating that they will cover numerous other candidates in the same non-partisan manner.

Readers should not assume that simply re-printing speeches is non-partisan:

Selecting which speeches to include is potentially partisan (the book has just one speech on religious values and three on abortion-related topics, but the numbers could have been switched at the editor's discretion);

Juxtaposing speeches is potentially partisan (a speech on Ronald Reagan is juxtaposed with a speech on "Defense and Peace," for example, emphasizing Santorum's association with Reagan's "peace through strength" doctrine);

Assigning chapter headings is potentially partisan (the chapter entitled "Sanctity of Marriage" might have been entitled "Anti-Gay Marriage" or "Heterosexual Marriage," for example).

At OnTheIssues, we make those same three types of choices

every day—so we are well aware of the potential partisanship in every selection we choose, every juxtaposition we make, and every headline we write. When we say the "Modern American Statesmen Series" accomplishes their task in a non-partisan manner, we mean they have successfully avoided introducing their own potential biases. We hope that OnTheIssues is viewed in the same manner.

There's nothing exciting in this book; it's just the basics, on all the key issues, from speeches made in the period 1995 through 2005. We look forward to more in the series, and will excerpt them when they become available.

Book review written Aug. 2011

We re-excerpted (and re-reviewed!) this book now that Sen. Santorum is one of the frontrunners in the 2012 GOP Primary.

The former Senator is a Christian conservative, which means he focuses very heavily on social and moral issues such as abortion, anti-gay marriage, and church-state issues. Santorum is also an economic conservative, meaning he believes in lower taxes and trickle-down economics. Michele Bachmann and Sarah Palin also fit that class of conservative.

As of today, the four frontrunners for the GOP nomination exemplify several other classes of conservatives. Ron Paul is a libertarian, which means he supports economic conservatism but not social conservatism (he supports gay rights, for example). Newt Gingrich shares most of the same views as Santorum, but focuses on economic conservatism. Hence Gingrich *sounds* less hard-core than Santorum on pro-life and anti-gay issues, but really the two agree on the issues, while disagreeing on what priority to assign them. Mitt Romney is a populist conservative, meaning he disagrees with Santorum both on priority and on some issues too.

Given that Gov. Romney is the GOP frontrunner and the other three top-tier candidates are vying for the non-Romney vote, Republican primary voters now face a clear choice: a libertarian conservative

(Rep. Paul); an economic conservative (Speaker Gingrich); or a social conservative (Sen. Santorum). Our two-dimensional political analysis, differentiating social issues from economic issues, clarifies these distinctions.

Book review written Jan. 2012;
full excerpts available online at:
www.ontheissues.org/Santorum_Speaks.htm

Book Review: Real Change:
From the World that Fails
to the World that Works
by Speaker Newt Gingrich
(Dec. 18, 2007)

The Republican Party has failed in implementing the Revolution of 1994, and it's time to restart that Revolution again (p. 71). At least, according to Newt Gingrich, who considers himself the architect of the Revolution of 1994. This book was written in 2009, so it's unclear whether Newt considers the Tea Party to be the new Revolution (his partner in the Revolution of 1994, Rep. Dick Armey, certainly does, as outlined in his 2010 book, Give Us Liberty). It is NOT unclear, however, that Newt considers himself to be the appropriate leader for the new Revolution.

The new Revolution is needed now, says Newt, because of the losses to Obama and the Democrats: "For a number of years I kept quiet, but the recent devastation to my party is now so great that I am compelled to speak out explicitly and decisively." (p. 24). He blames partisanship on both sides of the aisle (p. 43) for the dysfunctional state of American politics: he has one chapter entitled "An Unreformed Right: Why Republicans Can't Govern Successfully"; and another entitled "An Unreformed Left: Why Democrats Can't Deliver Real Change." The solution? Go back to the non-partisanship of the Revolution of 1994.

Citizens who actually remember the Revolution of 1994, in contrast to Newt, generally consider the era to be quite partisan. Newt DOES deserve credit for "nationalizing" the Congressional election of 1994 (getting people to vote for the Contract With America as much as just for their individual Congressional race); and he DOES deserve credit for a Revolution. But he also deserves blame for the harsh partisanship that characterized the House of Representatives in the 1990s, culminating in Bill Clinton's impeachment, arguably the most partisan act in American history. Citizens might also contrast Newt's view with the fact that he resigned from the House speakership in the wake of a government shutdown—also an intensely partisan act.

Nevertheless, Newt is back, and he is running for President. This book is just the first salvo in his battle for the GOP nomination. He has prepared appropriately: he formed several political organizations in the past decade to bolster his credentials on key issues (each of which gets a plug for its website, p. xxi):

- The Center for Health Transformation (www.HealthTransformation.net)

- American Solutions for Winning the Future (www.AmericanSolutions.com)

- Renewing American Leadership (ReAL, www.RenewingAmericanLeadership.com)

If Newt does enter the Republican primary, he is sure to be great entertainment. While Newt is renowned for his slightly non-mainstream academic analysis, listeners accept it as mainstream because he delivers it with such certitude (almost always in this book, the passive voice is used, to illustrate how it's obvious that most voters are in agreement). His analysis is data-driven and historical (he's a history professor, after all), although some might call that "wonkish," a sure-fire losing attitude since Dukakis' days. Newt would call his attitude "futuristic," since his hero is still Alvin Toffler, author of "Future Shock" and "The Third Wave" (p. 65).

Whether wonkish or futuristic, Newt will be non-mainstream and hence entertaining. For example, he proposes (in the passive voice) that the US should invade Pakistan: "Afghanistan would have been dealt with in a regional context that would have included the Waziristan section of Pakistan." (p. 305). And maybe invade Syria and others too (also in the passive voice): "There would have been no free passage through Damascus for foreign terrorists to come kill Americans," but that wouldn't actually require invasions because the dictators might yield once they saw "the fury of the American people mobilized to action."

In summary, Newt positions himself as the conservative choice:

more hawkish than the GOP hawks; more anti-Obama than the rest of the GOP; and more "change" than Obama ever offered. Newt will have a lot of trouble with the conservatives accepting his three divorces; he'll have even more trouble with the general electorate accepting his conversion to non-partisanship; and he'll have the most trouble of all with voters who remember him as the past generation instead of the future. But he'll be a heck of a lot of fun!

Book review written April 2011;
full excerpts available online at:
www.ontheissues.org/Real_Change.htm

Book Review:
Rediscovering God in America:
Reflections on the Role of Faith in Our Nation's History and Future
by Speaker Newt Gingrich
(Oct. 10, 2006)

Newt Gingrich in this book expresses strongly how important God has been to American history. The structure of this book is a "tour" of Washington DC, pointing out all of the references to God built into our public monuments and buildings, as well as in their design and history. The details of that aspect of the book are mostly omitted here because OnTheIssues doesn't have categories for history nor architecture.

But there is a political purpose too, and those comprise our excerpts. In particular, Gingrich applies the historical importance of God in America to examine numerous current public policy issues, from the Pledge of Allegiance to school prayer. Gingrich reserves particular venom for the US Supreme Court and other courts who rule in favor of omitting God from public displays—claiming that they are usurping power intended for the legislature, and also ignoring the importance of God in centuries of American history.

This book is similar in conclusions to Mike Huckabee's Character Makes a Difference. Gov. Huckabee, however, comes from a pastoral perspective, arguing on religious and moral grounds instead of Gingrich's historical grounds. Gingrich's argument is certainly more effective when attempting to persuade non-Christians or secularists.

This book is similar in conclusions to Mike Huckabee's Character Makes a Difference. Gov. Huckabee, however, comes from a pastoral perspective, arguing on religious and moral grounds instead of Gingrich's historical grounds. Gingrich's argument is certainly more effective when attempting to persuade non-Christians or secularists.

Book review written May 2007;
full excerpts available online at:
www.ontheissues.org/Rediscovering_God.htm

Santorum vs. Gingrich on VoteMatch

VoteMatch is our 20-question quiz which summarizes the candidate's views on the controversial issues of the day.

VoteMatch Social Issues

	Rick Santorum	Newt Gingrich
Abortion is a woman's right	strongly opposes	strongly opposes
Require companies to hire more women & minorities	favors	strongly opposes
Same-sex domestic partnership benefits	strongly opposes	opposes
Teacher-led prayer in public schools	strongly favors	strongly favors
Parents choose schools via vouchers	strongly favors	strongly favors

VoteMatch Domestic Issues

	Rick Santorum	Newt Gingrich
More federal funding for health coverage	strongly opposes	strongly opposes
Death Penalty	strongly favors	strongly favors
Mandatory Three Strikes sentencing laws	favors	favors
Absolute right to gun ownership	favors	favors
Drug use is immoral: enforce laws against it	strongly favors	strongly favors

VoteMatch Economic Issues

	Rick Santorum	Newt Gingrich
Privatize Social Security	strongly favors	strongly favors
Make taxes more progressive	strongly opposes	opposes
Stricter limits on political campaign funds	strongly opposes	strongly opposes
Allow churches to provide welfare services	favors	favors
Replace coal & oil with alternatives	strongly opposes	strongly opposes

VoteMatch International Issues

	Rick Santorum	Newt Gingrich
Illegal immigrants earn citizenship	strongly opposes	neutral
Support & expand free trade	strongly favors	favors
The Patriot Act harms civil liberties	strongly opposes	strongly opposes
Expand the armed forces	strongly favors	strongly favors
US out of Iraq and Afghanistan	strongly opposes	favors

In our online quiz, you fill in your answers for these 20 questions, and we match you against all the candidates. Please see:

http://quiz.ontheissues.org/

Afterword

We hope that this book encourages you, as voters, to make your decisions based on the issues. We recognize the reality of American politics: voters make their decisions based primarily on whether they like the candidates. Accordingly, our goal is to get voters to compare their issue preferences in comparison to candidate issue stances when considering which candidates to like.

We intentionally omitted from this book any biographical background on Sen. Santorum and Speaker Gingrich. Details of their birthplaces and religious affiliations—and minutiae of every other personal detail—are readily available in the mainstream media. Their issue stances are more challenging for voters to find. In the case of Santorum vs. Gingrich, their issue stances often coincide closely; they differ in their priorities or how they express their views in wider contexts. This book presents enough context, we hope, for you to make the distinction between these two similar candidates.

Why does the mainstream media fail at this important function? Because they are "news" organizations which are poorly suited to covering political campaigns. "News" implies reporting on what is "new": Gingrich's stance on drugs has not changed since 1998, and Santorum has not expressed any view on the death penalty since his vote in 1996, so there's nothing in the news about those issues. But if you are impassioned about the Drug War or the death penalty, you cannot rely on the news media for those non-newsworthy issues. And that's where we come in.

This book represents an archive of where these two candidates stand on the key issues of our time. We don't consider whether candidates' issue stances are new—just what they say on each issue. That often requires a lot of digging on our part!

Our online website www.ontheissues.org covers more issues than can fit in any book: more stances from Santorum and Gingrich, as well as all of the other 2012 candidates. We score each candidate on a 20-question quiz called "VoteMatch." A representation of the VoteMatch quiz results for the presidential contenders appears on the back cover of this book. The mainstream media interpret candidates using a one-dimensional "right-left" analysis. That simplistic analysis comes to nonsensical conclusions like calling Ron Paul "extreme right-wing" even though he opposes the Iraq War; opposes the PATRIOT Act; supports drug legalization; and supports same-sex domestic partnership benefits.

We find our two-dimensional analysis to be more accurate in differentiating candidates than that traditional one-dimensional analysis. We don't claim that our method is perfect—just superior to the simplistic mainstream media. VoteMatch uses a Social Issues dimension plus an Economic Issues dimension; we interpret candidates based on whether they believe in government involvement in either or both of those dimensions. Using the two-dimensional analysis differentiates five classes of political beliefs:

1. *Libertarian:*
   No government involvement in social issues
   No government involvement in economic issues

2. *Conservative:*
   Government involvement in social issues
   No government involvement in economic issues

3. *Liberal:*
   No government involvement in social issues
   Government involvement in economic issues

4. *Populist:*
   Government involvement in social issues
   Government involvement in economic issues

5. *Centrist:*
   Some government involvement in social issues
   Some government involvement in economic issues

Most importantly, you can answer the same 20 questions and see *your* political label and how the candidates match up with *you*. We invite you to try the VoteMatch quiz at:

http://quiz.ontheissues.org

Other Books in This Series

- Rick Perry vs. Mitt Romney On The Issues

- Ron Paul vs. Barack Obama On The Issues

- Sarah Palin vs. Michele Bachmann On The Issues

- Newt Gingrich vs. Ron Paul On The Issues

- Barack Obama vs. Mitt Romney On The Issues

About the Author

Jesse Gordon has been the editor-in-chief of OnTheIssues.org since its formation in 1999. His passion revolves around providing issue-based coverage on political races, to combat the mainstream media's growing lack of such coverage.

Mr. Gordon holds a Master's degree in Public Policy from Harvard University's Kennedy School of Government. He and the website OnTheIssues.org are based in Cambridge, Massachusetts. He resides with his fiancée, Kathleen; his son, Julien; Kathleen's son, Derek; their cat, Chanel; and six fish with whom Chanel is obsessed.

Mr. Gordon replies to email personally, at jesse@ontheissues.org— whether to suggest improvements to the website or to order one of the other books above. Most importantly, you can answer the same 20 questions and see your political label and how the candidates match up with you. We invite you to try the VoteMatch quiz at:

http://quiz.ontheissues.org

www.ingramcontent.com/pod-product-compliance
Lightning Source LLC
Chambersburg PA
CBHW061259280526
45784CB00002B/818